The Zucchini Cookbook

By Paula Simmons
Drawings by Ruth Richardson

Pacific Search Press

Cover and Page Design by Frederick Walsh

First edition
Copyright © 1974 by Pacific Search

Second edition, revised and enlarged
Copyright © 1975 by Pacific Search
Second printing 1976
Third printing 1978
International Standard Book Number 0-914718-10-X
Library of Congress Catalog Card Number 74-77037
Printed in the United States of America

TABLE OF CONTENTS

LAZT BUT NOT LEAZT . . .

It stands to reason that modern society will presume this modest volume that purports to be a zucchini-oriented cookbook is of ordinary consequence.

As my extremely subtle, learned grandmother (Nonno) might have said: "Ho! Ho!" (She didn't speak a word of English because she wanted her zucchini secrets to go with her to her grave. She did and they did.)

The truth is now, as they say, out. Or "in." It is time the historic legend of the zucchini is unfolded so that we may save this great, free country from the developing Food Crisis ahead. That's spelled high prices and scarcity.

Let me tell you a story. I am authorized, at last, to make this revelation by the international AWAZIHNCBAB compact — the Anybody With a Z in His Name Can't Be All Bad organization, founded by Zsa Zsa Gabor's Italian great-great grandfather, Bimbo, who fled from Italy to Hungary with the original planting instructions for zucchini. His real name was Zero, which lost everything in translation, so he switched to Bimbo because he had a cousin in San Francisco. Follow me?

The first zucchini seeds were handed down to the citizens of Abruzzi in East-Central Italy by Zarathrustra because they were, of course, the salt of the earth — and they had two Z's in their provincial name. At the same time, they were told to nurture the seeds and distribute them and their secret only to the common man and woman (chauvinism was a no-no). The gods would strike dead any zucchini worshiper breaking the law and turning over the heavenly food to the greedy, the licentious, the non-Italian.

For centuries no one broke the code of honor. Great men like Michelangelo, Dante, Boccaccio, Leonardo, Manzoni, and Verdi had many problems with the authorities. And do you know why? As native members of the Zecret Zucchini Zociety, they kept patches of the delectable plant in hidden yards, safe from the jealous, marauding nobility and carabinieri. Also, it was rumored they had found a way to smoke the stuff, but that intelligence died with them, fortunately.

The Italian Mafia was formed not for the reasons given in most history books. Sicilian Robin Hoods, indeed! Their real purpose was to crack the Z-Code.

As they and other interlopers knew, the zucchini was Italy's soul food, its principal sustenance, the food of, by, and for the gods. The wonderful Italian song, "O Sole Mio," is actually a careful corruption designed by Ze Underworld to protect the original, "O Zucchini Mio."

It was Chris Columbus, a member of the ZZ, who brought the zucchini seed and secret to the New World, despite the New World's longtime reputation as the land of plenty. Through the years from 1492 everyone was mum.

The first crack in the historic silence came when Al Capp (his real name is Alfredo Capucino, of course) grew so desperate for a new story line that he introduced the shmoo to his comic strip. Now, it can be told, the shmoo was actually the zucchini, made white and given human life to disguise its true identity. Remember how the shmoo smiled and loved everyone and, when destroyed, it simply multiplied? Like rabbit food, the shmoo grew and grew and grew. Like Big Z.

I have just returned from Abruzzi II, where the Zecret Zociety has granted permission to tell all and permit Paula Simmons to publish this book. Paula Simmons? Well, her real name, of course, is Paolina Zabaglione, but her parents ran into an illiterate clerk at the county division of birth and stuff statistics.

If you're not convinced yet of this gentle conspiracy, please note that the nize lady from Pacific Search who encouraged Paula and me and who is in charge of Special Publications (a likely story!) is Alice Seed. Scout's honor!

Paula knows, and Alice knows, and I know, and all good Italians know that the Italian soul food had to come out of hiding eventually in the Great Inflation (that's today, Sam), so the ZZ and the AWAZIHNCBAB are hereby dissolved in order that America can be saved.

Notice how Paolina Z for Simmons has cleverly given the recipes an international twist — Zucchini Tacos, Chinese Zucchini, Curried Zucchini (named after my good friend, Harold Curry, a true internationalist), and Zucchini Tetrazzini, made with Swiss cheese, no less, to throw the Mafiosi off the scent. But don't let her fool you. No matter how you spell it, chop it, fry it, broil it, saute it, swallow it, it still comes out Italian soul food. Summer squash, indeed!

Oh, yes, a few final notes. Before Al Capp for Capucino, an Italian immigrant named Arnoldo Z. Benedizio very nearly spilled the beans. Or the Z seeds, that is. It was he who invented the political speech. The best of his cliches was, of course, ". . . and now, last but not least . . ." Naturally, he was a gourmet and was thinking only of Big Z, the last of the alphabet.

Don't forget. When you have to make a run for it to the shelter, forget all the other stuff. Just bring along Paula's book, a package of zucchini seeds, and a very small shovel. And, when you plant those seeds, for goodness' sake, jump back quickly!

Louis R. Guzzo,
With 55 years of experience in eating
Executive Editor of the Seattle
Post-Intelligencer and contributor
of recipes on pages 76, 135, 136,
138, and the top of 139.

GROW IT

The zucchini is a very fast growing, prolific variety of summer squash. Since it is a compact, bushy plant, it is convenient for home gardeners. Its huge leaves make it highly ornamental but tend to hide some of the green fruits, so that even with daily inspection some squash will escape detection and grow to monster size. Ideally, they should be picked when immature; leaving too many to grow to huge sizes can slow down the blooming and production of new fruit. But there are some recipes for the escapees.

For an early crop, plant seeds indoors in compressed peat pots a few weeks before the average date of the last frost. Set the plants into the garden as soon as all danger of frost is past. When plants have their second set of leaves, if the weather is still too cool at night, you can either set them out and provide protection or transplant to a gallon can with drainage holes in the bottom. Set the can outside during the day and bring it in at night. Keep these small plants well watered, for low indoor humidity dries them out quickly.

For seeding directly into the soil, wait until danger of frost is past, then sow in hills or rows with well-rotted manure buried below them, five seeds to a hill, in hills four feet apart from center to center. These can be thinned to the strongest two or three plants. When plants are well established, a heavy straw mulch around them will keep down the weeds and conserve moisture. Zucchini need a lot of water at the roots, but not on the crown of the plant or on the immature fruits. If the soil is poor and water tends to run off instead of soak in, make a trench-and-dike arrangement for watering or sink a large can with lots of drainage holes in the bottom next to the squash plants while they are small. Fill the can with water and it will slowly drain into the soil by the squash roots.

Most zucchini varieties take only 40 to 55 days for the first little squash to be ready to eat. (Winter squash, by comparison, take from 100 to 125 days.) The fruits develop from the bright yellow female blossoms, which are low on short stems. These are pollinated from the yellow male blossoms, which are on long upright stems. It is estimated that three hills of zucchini will amply supply a family of four if you keep the fruits picked to encourage more bearing. Zucchini will keep for several days in the refrigerator. At the end of the season let a few grow to monster size; pick them and store in a cool place as you would winter squash and the zucchini will keep until December.

There are many good varieties available, but we were particularly impressed with the new hybrid Aristocrat zucchini, a 1973 "All American" winner. It is quick to mature, with first fruits ready within 48 days of sowing seed directly into the garden, and is very prolific with a good keeping quality. Developed by the Peto Seed Company in California, it will be available from W. Atlee Burpee Company and a number of other sources. The new Burpee Golden zucchini is worth some garden space for its attractive bright yellow color, but it is no match for the Aristocrat in either taste or production. Beautini from Jung Seed Company and Elite from Harris Seed Company are two other early hybrids that are more satisfactory. And for fun and a conversation piece, Nichols Garden Nursery has seeds for two tasty novelties — a round zucchini shaped like a small cantaloupe, and Courese, a white one from France which is firm-meated with very few seeds.

For a plentiful supply of zucchini in spring, summer, and fall, GROW IT!

AND COOK IT!

WHAT CAN I DO WITH A BIG ZUCCHINI? A common lament of home gardeners and their friends. This book has dozens of answers. Many recipes are created especially for the king-size zucchini, the one that remains hidden under those beautiful big squash leaves until it seems much too huge for cooking, valuable only as a conversation piece.

HOW CAN I GET MY CHILDREN TO EAT VEGETABLES? The blues song of mothers everywhere. They don't like zucchini? Perhaps they don't like the way it is prepared. Try irresistible chocolate zucchini cake, pineapple zucchini cookies, zucchalmond squares, zucchini tacos, zucchini a la maddalena, Swiss steak with invisible zucchini, cream of zucchini soup, zucchini dill pickles, or some old favorites like the popular zucchini breads. If you think it can only be served boiled with salt and pepper, try THE ZUCCHINI COOKBOOK!

My cooking instructions are sometimes casual. Baking measurements are always given for unsifted flour, and dry ingredients are usually just mixed instead of sifted together. In all my recipes this seems to work just fine. The cake recipes are very easy. Most need no frosting and are cut-in-the-pan cakes that offer the appeal of cake with the convenience of bar cookies.

Some recipes suggest a Teflon utensil because less liquid is required when using a nonstick finish and less oil is needed to saute, fry, or brown food. My own use of nonstick skillets started with an aversion to pot scrubbing. If you are not using Teflon, you may need to add a trifle more liquid or fat to some recipes, and stir a bit more, too.

I often say "steam" the zucchini. If you don't have a vegetable steamer (a little perforated basket on legs that fits inside any saucepan with a lid), it is a worthwhile investment, a versatile kitchen helper, and useful for many other vegetables when liquid will not be used as part of the recipe.

A note on calories of some cooked vegetables:

calories per pound

Zucchini	74
Cabbage	109
Spinach	115
Carrots	138
Beets	187
Peas	300-400

depending on maturity

BREADS

DIPS

SPREADS

LIGHT ZUCCHINI BREAD

EGGS   3 whole
VEGETABLE OIL   3/4 cup
SUGAR   1-1/2 cups
POWDERED LEMON PEEL   1 teaspoon
ORANGE EXTRACT   1/2 teaspoon
VANILLA   1/4 teaspoon
ZUCCHINI   2 cups grated (can be firm flesh of very large
            one, peeled if peeling is tough)
FLOUR   2-1/2 cups, unsifted (or more*)
SALT   3/4 teaspoon
CINNAMON   1/2 teaspoon
GINGER   1/4 teaspoon
SODA   1 teaspoon
BAKING POWDER   2 teaspoons
NUTS   1/2 cup chopped

Beat EGGS; add OIL and SUGAR; beat well. Add flavoring and ZUCCHINI; beat. Mix dry ingredients together; stir in and add NUTS; mix well. Bake in small loaf pans or in oiled cans (size #2-1/2) at 350° for 1 hour. Cool in cans until bread will remove easily, then cool on wire rack. This freezes well and is an ideal way to use up those monsters.

You may need more flour if using small or medium size zucchini that have more moisture. If using very large zucchini, discard the center pulp. The firm flesh is not extra moist, but perfect for this recipe.

DARK ZUCCHINI BREAD

EGGS   3 whole

VEGETABLE OIL   1 cup

BROWN SUGAR   2 cups, firmly packed

VANILLA   3 teaspoons

ZUCCHINI   3 cups grated (can be firm flesh of very large
            one, peeled if peeling is tough)

MOLASSES   1 tablespoon

FLOUR   4 cups, unsifted

SALT   1 teaspoon

SODA   1 teaspoon

BAKING POWDER   1/4 teaspoon

CINNAMON   2 teaspoons

PUMPKIN PIE SPICE   1 teaspoon

NUTS   1/2 cup chopped

Beat EGGS; add OIL and BROWN SUGAR; beat well. Add VANILLA, grated ZUCCHINI, and MOLASSES; beat. Mix dry ingredients together; add NUTS and beat well. Bake in greased and floured small loaf pans or in 3 oiled cans (size #2-1/2) at 350° for 1 hour. Cool in cans until bread will remove easily, then cool on rack.

Note: This freezes well. To freeze in cans, cool bread completely, then return it to can; top with double layer of foil tied securely over top of can.

CHOCOLATE ZUCCHINI BREAD

EGGS   3 whole
VEGETABLE OIL   1 cup
BROWN SUGAR   2 cups firmly packed
VANILLA   1 teaspoon
ZUCCHINI   3 cups grated (can be firm flesh of very large one,
            peeled if peeling is tough)
BAKER'S UNSWEETENED CHOCOLATE   2 squares, melted
FLOUR   4 cups unsifted
SALT   1 teaspoon
SODA   1 teaspoon
BAKING POWDER   1/4 teaspoon
CINNAMON   1 teaspoon
PUMPKIN PIE SPICE   1 teaspoon
NUTS   1/2 cup chopped

Beat EGGS; add OIL and BROWN SUGAR; beat well. Add VANILLA, ZUCCHINI, AND CHOCOLATE; beat. Mix dry ingredients together; add NUTS and beat well. Bake in 6 tiny greased loaf pans, or in 2 standard loaf pans at 350° for 40 to 60 minutes, depending on loaf size. Cool in pans until bread will remove easily, then cool on rack.

BRAN BREAD

FLOUR   2 cups, unsifted
BAKING POWDER   2 teaspoons
SALT   1/2 teaspoon
SODA   1/2 teaspoon
SUGAR   1/3 cup
ALLSPICE   3/4 teaspoon
BRAN FLAKES   1 cup
NUTS   1/2 cup chopped
EGG   1 whole, beaten
BUTTERMILK   1-1/4 cups
SHORTENING   3 tablespoons, melted
ZUCCHINI   1 cup diced (can be from large one)

Mix together FLOUR, BAKING POWDER, SALT, SODA, SUGAR, and ALLSPICE; add BRAN FLAKES and NUTS. Combine EGG with BUTTERMILK and melted SHORTENING; add to dry ingredients and beat just enough to mix well. Stir in ZUCCHINI. Bake in greased and floured 9 x 5 x 3-inch loaf pan at 350° approximately 50 to 60 minutes. A very moist bread; cuts best when cool.

ZUCCHINI KUCHEN

EGG   1 whole, plus WATER to make 2/3 cup
ONION   2 tablespoons grated
BISCUIT MIX   2-1/4 cups
ZUCCHINI   1 medium
MAYONNAISE
POPPY SEEDS

Break EGG into measuring cup and add WATER to fill to 2/3 cup mark. Add this to ONION and BISCUIT MIX; stir with fork. Turn out, knead lightly, and pat into oiled 9-inch round pan. Slice ZUCCHINI in 3/8-inch rounds; arrange slices overlapping on top of dough. Spread tops thickly with MAYONNAISE. Sprinkle with POPPY SEEDS. Bake at 425° for 25 to 30 minutes. Serves 6.

Any leftovers can be reheated in foil and are just as tasty.

PANCAKES

EGG   1 whole
FLOUR   1/2 cup, unsifted
SALT   1/8 teaspoon
SUGAR   1 teaspoon
ZUCCHINI   1 cup grated (can be from large one)

Beat EGG well. Mix FLOUR, SALT, and SUGAR together; sift over ZUCCHINI and fold this into the EGG. Drop from tablespoon on greased griddle; flatten with back of spoon. Cook until golden brown; turn and brown other side. Cook until done through. Good with honey or syrup.

MUFFINS

FLOUR   2 cups
SALT   3/4 teaspoon
BAKING POWDER   2 teaspoons
SUGAR   3 tablespoons
MACE   1/8 teaspoon ground
BUTTER or MARGARINE   2 tablespoons
ZUCCHINI   1 cup finely chopped
EGG   1 whole
MILK   1/2 cup
CINNAMON   1/2 teaspoon
SUGAR   1 tablespoon

Mix *FLOUR, SALT, BAKING POWDER, SUGAR, and MACE. Cut in BUTTER with pastry blender or fork. Add ZUCCHINI; mix. Add EGG beaten lightly with MILK. Spoon into greased muffin tins. Mix CINNAMON and SUGAR and sprinkle on top of muffin batter. Bake at 400° approximately 20 minutes.*

CRACKER TOPPERS OR DIPS

CHILI SAUCE   1/4 cup
MAYONNAISE   1/4 cup
PREPARED HORSERADISH   1 tablespoon
ZUCCHINI   1/2 cup chopped

Mix and chill.

DEVILED HAM SPREAD   1 2-1/4-ounce can
PREPARED MUSTARD   1 teaspoon
WORCESTERSHIRE SAUCE   1 teaspoon
ZUCCHINI   1/2 cup shredded and drained

Mix and chill.

SHARP CHEESE   1 cup shredded
ZUCCHINI   1 cup finely chopped
WALNUTS   1/2 cup chopped
MAYONNAISE   3/4 cup

Mix and chill.

MARGARINE   1/2 cup, soft
ZUCCHINI   3 tablespoons chopped
CARROT   1 tablespoon grated
CELERY   1 tablespoon finely chopped
GREEN PEPPER   1 tablespoon chopped
SEASONED SALT   1 teaspoon

Mix and chill.

SHARP CHEESE   sliced and cut in squares
DILL PICKLES   sliced crossways
ZUCCHINI   small, sliced crossways

Top crackers with slice of PICKLE, slice of ZUCCHINI, and slice of CHEESE; broil until cheese melts.

Several small ZUCCHINI, centers removed with apple corer. Stuff with mixture of:

CREAM CHEESE   4 ounces, softened
BACON   2 slices, crumbled
GARLIC SALT   to taste

Chill. Slice crossways and serve on crackers spread with mayonnaise.

ONION   1 tablespoon chopped
ZUCCHINI   1 cup chopped
TOMATO SAUCE   2/3 cup
HOT PEPPER SAUCE   5 drops
CREAM CHEESE   4 ounces, cut in chunks
DILL PICKLE   1, finely chopped

Simmer ONION, ZUCCHINI, TOMATO SAUCE, and HOT PEPPER SAUCE for 15 to 20 minutes. Put in blender container with CREAM CHEESE; blend until very smooth. Stir in chopped DILL PICKLE. Chill until ready to serve.

ZUCCHINI   1 cup grated (can be firm flesh of large one)
PLAIN YOGURT   3 tablespoons
SEASONED SALT   1/4 teaspoon
GARLIC POWDER   1/4 teaspoon
FREEZE-DRIED SHALLOTS   1 teaspoon (or 1/2 teaspoon
chopped FRESH SHALLOTS)
PAPRIKA   to garnish

Drain ZUCCHINI in colander. Press between towels to drain off more liquid. Combine with YOGURT, seasonings, and SHALLOTS. Garnish with a sprinkle of PAPRIKA. Chill well.

CAKES

COOKIES

DESSERTS

EASY ZUCCHINI PINEAPPLE JELLYROLL CAKE

CRUSHED PINEAPPLE   1 cup, drained
ZUCCHINI   1-1/4 cups finely diced (can be firm flesh of a very
      large one, peeled)
BROWN SUGAR   1/2 cup firmly packed
SUGAR   1/2 cup
EGGS   3, separated
PINEAPPLE JUICE   2 tablespoons
PINEAPPLE EXTRACT   1/4 teaspoon
FLOUR   1 cup unsifted
SALT   1/4 teaspoon
BAKING POWDER   1 teaspoon
POWDERED SUGAR
WHIPPED CREAM

Drain PINEAPPLE well and save the juice. Sprinkle PINEAPPLE in greased 9 × 13 × 2-inch pan. (Smaller pan makes the roll too thick.) Scatter ZUCCHINI over PINEAPPLE. Sprinkle with BROWN SUGAR and pat it down with your hand.

Mix SUGAR and EGG yolks. Stir in PINEAPPLE JUICE and EXTRACT, then FLOUR, SALT, and BAKING POWDER. Beat EGG whites until stiff, fold into batter. Spoon batter over ZUCCHINI mixture in pan, smooth the top. Bake at 375° for 15 to 18 minutes, or until cake tests done. DO NOT OVERBAKE.

Loosen cake from sides of pan. Turn it out, upside down, on clean dishtowel sprinkled with POWDERED SUGAR. Trim off any crisp edges of cake. While still hot, roll the cake, starting at the 9-inch end (pick up edge of cloth to start it rolling). Wrap it in the cloth until it is cool. Slice and top with whipped cream for an elegant dessert. Best eaten the day you bake it.

MOLASSES CAKE

EGG   1 whole, beaten
SUGAR   1/3 cup
MOLASSES   1/2 cup
SHORTENING   1/4 cup, melted
NUTS   1/2 cup chopped
FLOUR   2 cups, unsifted
SALT   1 teaspoon
SODA   1 teaspoon
BAKING POWDER   3/4 teaspoon
DRY LEMON PEEL   1-1/2 teaspoons grated
SOUR MILK   2/3 cup*
ZUCCHINI   2 cups finely diced, not grated (can be firm
            flesh of very large one)

Mix EGG, SUGAR, MOLASSES, and SHORTENING; add NUTS. Mix together FLOUR, SALT, SODA, BAKING POWDER, and LEMON PEEL; add alternately with SOUR MILK. Stir in chopped ZUCCHINI. Bake in greased and floured 9 x 13-inch pan at 350° for 35 to 40 minutes. This is a moist cake, good with whipped cream or sweetened cream cheese frosting.

*To make sour milk, add 1 teaspoon lemon juice to 1/2 cup whole or skim milk. Let stand 5 minutes before using.

CHOCOLATE ZUCCHINI CAKE

MARGARINE   1/2 cup, soft
VEGETABLE OIL   1/2 cup
SUGAR   1-3/4 cups
EGGS   2 whole
VANILLA   1 teaspoon
SOUR MILK   1/2 cup*
FLOUR   2-1/2 cups, unsifted
COCOA   4 tablespoons
BAKING POWDER   1/2 teaspoon
BAKING SODA   1 teaspoon
CINNAMON   1/2 teaspoon
CLOVES   1/2 teaspoon
ZUCCHINI   2 cups finely diced, not shredded (works best
    with firm flesh of very large one)
CHOCOLATE CHIPS   1/4 cup

Cream *MARGARINE, OIL,* and *SUGAR. Add EGGS, VANILLA, and SOUR MILK;* beat with mixer. Mix together all the dry ingredients and add to creamed mixture; beat well with mixer. Stir in diced *ZUCCHINI.* Spoon batter into greased and floured 9 x 12 x 2-inch pan; sprinkle top with *CHOCOLATE CHIPS.* Bake at 325° for 40 to 45 minutes or until toothpick or cake tester comes out clean and dry. This really needs no frosting; it is moist and very tender.

Tip: *To finely dice large zucchini, slice it crosswise in 1/4-inch slices. Take each slice, chop it in half, and remove and discard center half-moon of pulp and seeds. The remaining half circle of firm flesh, 1/4-inch thick, can be easily diced into 1/4-inch cubes. If skin is tender it will not need to be peeled.*

*To make sour milk, add 1 teaspoon lemon juice to 1/2 cup whole or skim milk. Let stand 5 minutes before using.

FRUITCAKE

ZUCCHINI   1 cup diced, not shredded
BRANDY FLAVORING   1 teaspoon
SUGAR   1 cup
APPLE JUICE   1 cup
MARGARINE   1/3 cup
WATER   2 tablespoons
DATES   1/2 cup chopped
BRANDY FLAVORING   1 teaspoon
FLOUR   2 cups, unsifted
SALT   1 teaspoon
BAKING POWDER   1 teaspoon
SODA   1 teaspoon
MIXED CANDIED FRUITS   1/2 cup
NUTS   1/2 cup chopped

Sprinkle diced ZUCCHINI with BRANDY FLAVORING; set aside. Combine SUGAR, APPLE JUICE, MARGARINE, WATER, and DATES; bring to boil. Boil 2 minutes; cool. Add BRANDY FLAVORING. Mix together FLOUR, SALT, BAKING POWDER, and SODA; stir into apple juice mixture. Add ZUCCHINI, CANDIED FRUITS, and NUTS; mix well. Spoon into 2 greased and paper-lined 9 x 5 x 3-inch loaf pans. Bake at 325° for 1 hour or until it tests done. Cool and chill before cutting.

ZUCCHINISAUCE CAKE

YELLOW or GREEN ZUCCHINI   3 cups cubed (can be
firm flesh of large one)
FROZEN APPLE JUICE   1/2 cup, undiluted
MARGARINE   1/2 cup, soft
SUGAR   1-1/2 cups
EGG   1 whole
FLOUR   2-1/2 cups, unsifted
SODA   1-1/2 teaspoons
SALT   1 teaspoon
CLOVES   1/2 teaspoon
ALLSPICE   1/2 teaspoon
CINNAMON   1/4 teaspoon
FROZEN APPLE JUICE   1/2 cup, thawed
WALNUTS   1/2 cup chopped

Simmer ZUCCHINI in frozen APPLE JUICE until tender. Whirl in blender;
set aside. Cream MARGARINE, SUGAR, and EGG until fluffy. Add
blended ZUCCHINI sauce; mix well. Mix together FLOUR, SODA, SALT,
and spices; add alternately with concentrated APPLE JUICE. Beat well.
Stir in NUTS. Bake in greased and floured 9 x 13 x 2-inch pan, at 350°
approximately 40 minutes. Frost as desired.

HONEY CAKE

MARGARINE   1/2 cup, soft
VANILLA   1 teaspoon
EGGS   2 whole
HONEY   2/3 cup
WATER   1/2 cup
FLOUR   1-3/4 cups unsifted
BAKING SODA   1 teaspoon
BAKING POWDER   1/2 teaspoon
SALT   1/2 teaspoon
ZUCCHINI   1 cup finely diced
NUTS   1/2 cup chopped (or 1/2 cup ground SUNFLOWER
*   SEEDS)*

Combine MARGARINE, VANILLA, EGGS, and HONEY; beat with mixer. Beat in WATER. Add dry ingredients; mix well. Stir in ZUCCHINI and NUTS. Bake at 350° in greased and floured 9 × 13 × 2-inch pan for 25 to 30 minutes, or until cake tests done. Good with sweetened cream cheese or topped with fruit.

SOURDOUGH ZUCCHINI CAKE

SHORTENING   1/2 cup
SUGAR   2 cups
EGGS   2 whole
SOURDOUGH STARTER   1-1/2 cups
ZUCCHINI   1-1/2 cups grated
CINNAMON   2-1/2 teaspoons
CLOVES   1 teaspoon
ALLSPICE   1 teaspoon
SALT   1-1/2 teaspoons
BAKING SODA   1-1/2 teaspoons
SUGAR   2 tablespoons
FLOUR   2 cups unsifted
WHITE RAISINS   1/2 cup
WALNUTS   1/2 cup chopped

Cream SHORTENING and SUGAR; beat in EGGS. Stir in SOURDOUGH STARTER, ZUCCHINI, and spices. Mix SALT, SODA, and SUGAR; sprinkle over batter, and stir in. Add FLOUR and stir until smooth; add RAISINS and WALNUTS, stir well. Pour into greased and floured 9 × 13 × 2-inch pan. Bake at 350° for 35 to 40 minutes, or until it tests done. Frost with very thin lemon glaze icing.

Lemon Glaze Icing

Melt 2 tablespoons MARGARINE; beat in 2 cups sifted POWDERED SUGAR, 1 tablespoon BOILING WATER, and 2 tablespoons LEMON JUICE.

UPSIDE-DOWN GINGERBREAD

MARGARINE   1/4 cup

BROWN SUGAR   3/4 cup firmly packed

ZUCCHINI   1-1/2 cups diced (can be firm flesh of very large
one, peeled and center pulp removed)

UNSWEETENED COCONUT   1 cup shredded or grated

VEGETABLE OIL   1/3 cup

EGG   1 whole

MOLASSES   1/2 cup

HONEY   1/2 cup

SOUR MILK or BUTTERMILK   1 cup

FLOUR   2-1/2 cups unsifted

GINGER   2 teaspoons

CINNAMON   1/2 teaspoon

BAKING SODA   1-3/4 teaspoons

SALT   1/2 teaspoon

ZUCCHINI   1/2 cup finely diced

*Grease sides of 9 × 13 × 2-inch pan (or two 8 × 8-inch pans). Melt
MARGARINE in bottom of pan or divide for 2 pans. Spread BROWN
SUGAR over. Mix ZUCCHINI and COCONUT together, layer over BROWN
SUGAR, and pat down gently with your hands.*

Gingerbread batter: *Mix together OIL, EGG, MOLASSES, and HONEY;
beat. Add SOUR MILK and beat. Add dry ingredients; beat well. Stir in
ZUCCHINI. Pour batter over ZUCCHINI COCONUT layer and spread
carefully. Bake at 350° for approximately 25 to 35 minutes or until it tests
done. Turn out on platter while hot. This is a moist cake with frostinglike
topping.*

WHITE CAKE

VEGETABLE OIL   1/4 cup

MARGARINE   1/4 cup, soft

SUGAR   1 cup

FLOUR   2 cups, unsifted

CORNSTARCH   2 tablespoons

BAKING POWDER   3 teaspoons

MILK   2/3 cup (can be skim milk)

ZUCCHINI   1 cup finely chopped, not grated

ALMOND EXTRACT   1/2 teaspoon

LEMON PEEL   1/2 teaspoon grated

EGG WHITES   3

Cream OIL and MARGARINE; add SUGAR and beat until fluffy. Mix together FLOUR, CORNSTARCH, and BAKING POWDER. Add alternately* with MILK to the creamed mixture; beat until smooth. Add ALMOND EXTRACT and LEMON PEEL. Stir in ZUCCHINI. Beat EGG WHITES stiff; fold into batter. Bake in 2 greased and floured 9-inch layer pans or sheet pan, at 375° for 25 to 30 minutes.

*Cake will be lighter in texture if dry ingredients are sifted into creamed mixture.

Zucchini Wedding Cake Decoration

Make double recipe of your favorite boiled or powdered sugar icing. Divide into three bowls—2/3 of icing in 1 bowl, the rest divided into 2 smaller bowls. With vegetable coloring, tint large bowl of icing a pale green, tint other 2 bowls of icing medium green and dark green. Spread tops and sides of all cake layers with pale green; decorate with other 2 shades of green by hand or with pastry tube.

Candy (using method from Zucchini Pie recipe) thin slices of small zucchini; twist each slice a little and stick into frosting around top edges of each layer. Place zucchini slices flat against frosted sides of layers and frosting rosettes against centers of slices.

Put layers together, tier style, with small zucchini (cut the same length) used as supporting pillars. Rest upper layers on rounds of white cardboard, cut to size of layers, and zucchini pillars will not poke up into layer above. Rest bottom of each zucchini pillar on a toothpick laid horizontally to keep it from sinking into layer below; frosting covers toothpick. To anchor, insert 1 toothpick vertically halfway up into bottom of each pillar and other half into layer beneath.

COFFEE BARS

FLOUR   1/2 cup, unsifted
BAKING POWDER   1 teaspoon
SALT   1/2 teaspoon
SUGAR   3/4 cup
EGG   1 whole
INSTANT COFFEE   1 tablespoon, dissolved in
WATER   1 teaspoon, hot
ZUCCHINI   1 cup peeled and diced (can be from large one)
NUTS   1/2 cup chopped

Mix together FLOUR, BAKING POWDER, SALT, and SUGAR. Add EGG, COFFEE, and ZUCCHINI; mix well. Stir in chopped NUTS. Spread in greased and floured 8 x 8-inch pan; bake at 350° for 25 minutes. Cut into bars when cool.

SWEETIES (with baked-on icing)

SUGAR   2/3 cup
MARGARINE   2 tablespoons
EGG   1 whole
FLOUR   1-1/2 cups, unsifted
BAKING POWDER   1 teaspoon
SALT   1/8 teaspoon
MILK   2/3 cup
ZUCCHINI   3/4 cup diced, not shredded

Beat SUGAR, MARGARINE, and EGG together. Mix dry ingredients together; add alternately with MILK. Stir in ZUCCHINI; mix well. Spread very thin on a greased and floured cookie sheet. Bake at 350° until lightly browned and cake tests done. Pour icing (below) over cake while hot; bake at 400° until top begins to bubble. Remove and cool; cut into squares.

Icing

BROWN SUGAR   9 tablespoons, firmly packed
CREAM or MILK   2 tablespoons
MARGARINE   4 tablespoons
SALT   pinch
VANILLA   1 teaspoon
COCONUT and/or NUTS   1/2 cup chopped (or mixture of
                both)

Cook SUGAR, MILK, and MARGARINE over low heat until thick. Add SALT, VANILLA, COCONUT, and/or NUTS. Pour over cake as instructed above.

CINNAMON ZUCCHINI BROWNIES

MARGARINE   1/3 cup, soft
BROWN SUGAR   1 cup, firmly packed
EGG   1 whole
VANILLA   1-1/2 teaspoons
FLOUR   1 cup, unsifted
CINNAMON   1-1/2 teaspoons
BAKING POWDER   1/4 teaspoon
SALT   1/2 teaspoon
NUTMEG   1/4 teaspoon
ZUCCHINI   1 cup chopped, not shredded (can be firm
               flesh of very large one)
NUTS   1/2 cup chopped

Mix MARGARINE and BROWN SUGAR; beat until fluffy. Add EGG and VANILLA; beat well. Add mixed dry ingredients and stir. Add ZUCCHINI and NUTS; mix. Bake in greased and floured 9 x 9-inch pan at 350° for 25 to 30 minutes. Cool in pan; cut into bars.

BLOND BROWNIES

MARGARINE   1/3 cup
WATER   1 tablespoon, hot
BROWN SUGAR   1 cup, firmly packed
EGG   1 whole
VANILLA   1 teaspoon
FLOUR   1 cup, unsifted
BAKING POWDER   1 teaspoon
SODA   1/8 teaspoon
SALT   1/2 teaspoon
ZUCCHINI   3/4 cup peeled and diced, not shredded (can be
          firm flesh of very large one)
NUTS   1/2 cup chopped
BUTTERSCOTCH CHIPS   1/4 cup

In large pan melt MARGARINE with hot WATER; add BROWN SUGAR and beat well. Cool. Add EGG and VANILLA; beat. Mix dry ingredients together and add to sugar mixture. Stir in ZUCCHINI and NUTS. Pour mixture into greased and floured 9 x 9-inch pan; sprinkle with BUTTERSCOTCH CHIPS. Bake at 350° for 20 to 25 minutes. Cool in pan: cut into bars.

ZUCCHALMOND SQUARES

ZUCCHINI   1-1/2 cups peeled and finely chopped
ALMOND EXTRACT   1 teaspoon
EGG WHITES   2
SUGAR   1/3 cup
FLOUR   1/2 cup, unsifted
BAKING POWDER   1 teaspoon
SALT   1/4 teaspoon
NUTS   1/2 cup chopped

Sprinkle chopped ZUCCHINI with ALMOND EXTRACT; set aside. Beat EGG WHITES until foamy; add SUGAR and beat thoroughly with electric mixer. Mix together dry ingredients and add; fold in NUTS and ZUCCHINI. Spoon into greased 8 x 8-inch pan. Bake at 350° for 40 minutes. Cool in pan; cut into squares.

ORANGE ZUCCHINI SQUARES

SUGAR   1 cup
FLOUR   1-1/2 cups, unsifted
SODA   1 teaspoon
SALT   1/2 teaspoon
CINNAMON   1 teaspoon
BAKING POWDER   1 teaspoon
NUTS   1/2 cup chopped
ZUCCHINI   1 cup grated, drained
EGG WHITES   2, lightly beaten
FROZEN ORANGE JUICE   1/2 cup, thawed
VEGETABLE OIL   4 tablespoons
ORANGE PEEL   1-1/2 teaspoons grated

Mix dry ingredients together; stir in NUTS and ZUCCHINI. To beaten EGG WHITES add the ORANGE JUICE and OIL. Fold into dry ingredients and add ORANGE PEEL. Spoon into greased and floured 9 x 13 x 2-inch pan. Bake at 350° for 40 to 45 minutes or until toothpick inserted in center comes out dry and clean. Cool; cut into squares. Can be drizzled with thin orange icing if desired.

FROSTED COOKIE FAVORITE

MARGARINE   1/2 cup, soft
BROWN SUGAR   1 cup, firmly packed
SUGAR   1/2 cup
EGGS   2 whole
CANNED MILK   1 cup, undiluted
VANILLA   1 teaspoon
FLOUR   2-2/3 cups, unsifted
SODA   1/2 teaspoon
WALNUTS   1 cup chopped
ZUCCHINI   1 cup diced, not shredded

Mix MARGARINE and sugars; beat. Add EGGS; mix well. Stir in CANNED MILK and VANILLA. Mix FLOUR and SODA together; stir in. Add NUTS. Chill 1 hour. Stir in ZUCCHINI, mixing well. Drop from tablespoon 2 inches apart on greased cookie sheet. Bake at 375° for 8 to 10 minutes, until delicately brown. Do not over-bake. While warm, frost and garnish with pieces of nut.

Butter Glaze Frosting

Melt 2 tablespoons MARGARINE; beat in 2 cups sifted POWDERED SUGAR and 1/4 cup undiluted CANNED MILK.

LEMON COOKIES

MARGARINE   1/2 cup
SUGAR   1/2 cup
HONEY   1/2 cup
EGG   1 whole
LEMON RIND   2 teaspoons grated
FLOUR   2 cups, unsifted
SALT   1/2 teaspoon
BAKING POWDER   1 teaspoon
ZUCCHINI   1 cup chopped, not shredded
WHEAT GERM   1 cup

Beat MARGARINE, SUGAR, and HONEY together until fluffy. Add EGG and LEMON RIND; beat well. Mix together FLOUR, SALT, and BAKING POWDER; stir into sugar mixture. Add ZUCCHINI and 1/2 cup of the WHEAT GERM. Refrigerate one hour or longer. If dough is not quite stiff enough to roll into balls, add more WHEAT GERM (some zucchini have more moisture than others, and would need this). Shape dough into 1-inch balls; roll balls in remaining 1/2 cup WHEAT GERM. Place on ungreased cookie sheet; flatten slightly. Place on oven rack above center of oven; bake at 400° for 8 minutes or until edges of cookies are just lightly browned. Remove to wire racks to cool. Store in covered cookie jar. Makes 5 dozen.

COUNTRY COOKIES

MARGARINE   1/2 cup, soft
SUGAR   1 cup
EGG   1 whole
FLOUR   1-1/2 cups, unsifted
SALT   1/2 teaspoon
BAKING SODA   1/2 teaspoon
CINNAMON   1 teaspoon
ALLSPICE   1/2 teaspoon
POTATO FLAKES   1-3/4 cups dry crushed
NUTS   1/2 cup chopped
ZUCCHINI   1 cup diced, not shredded
MILK   1/4 cup

Beat MARGARINE, SUGAR, and EGG together until fluffy. Mix together
FLOUR, SALT, SODA, and spices. Stir POTATO FLAKES, NUTS, and
ZUCCHINI into flour mixture; add to sugar mixture alternately with MILK.
Mix well after each addition. Drop from teaspoon on greased cookie sheet.
Bake at 350° for 12 to 14 minutes. Cool on brown paper. Makes about 4
dozen.

PINEAPPLE COOKIES

VEGETABLE OIL   1/2 cup
MARGARINE   1/2 cup, soft
BROWN SUGAR   2 cups, firmly packed
EGGS   2 whole
FROZEN PINEAPPLE JUICE   2 tablespoons
PINEAPPLE EXTRACT   1/2 teaspoon
VANILLA   1/4 teaspoon
ZUCCHINI   1 cup grated (can be firm flesh of very large
                one)
FLOUR   3 cups, unsifted
WHEAT GERM   1 cup
SODA   1/2 teaspoon
BAKING POWDER   1 teaspoon
SALT   1/2 teaspoon
QUICK-COOKING OATMEAL (not instant)   3/4 cup,
                                    uncooked

Cream OIL, MARGARINE, and SUGAR. Add EGGS; mix well by hand or
with mixer. Add PINEAPPLE JUICE and flavorings; beat. Stir in grated
ZUCCHINI. Mix dry ingredients except OATMEAL together; add to
creamed mixture; stir until all are moistened. Add OATMEAL; mix. Chill
dough for 20 minutes; drop from teaspoon onto greased cookie sheet. Bake at
350° for 10 minutes. Remove from cookie sheet at once; cool on brown
paper.

UPSIDE-DOWN PUDDING

FLOUR   1 tablespoon
POWDERED ORANGE PEEL   1 teaspoon
CINNAMON   1 teaspoon
ZUCCHINI   3 cups peeled and cut in 1/4-inch cubes
HONEY   1/2 cup
LEMON JUICE   1/2 teaspoon

Topping

FLOUR   1 cup, unsifted
BAKING POWDER   2 teaspoons
SALT   1/2 teaspoon
MARGARINE   1/4 cup, soft
EGG   1 whole
MILK   3 tablespoons
HONEY   2 tablespoons

Mix FLOUR, ORANGE PEEL, and CINNAMON with diced ZUCCHINI; stir in HONEY and LEMON JUICE. Spoon into oiled 8 x 8-inch pan.
Topping: Mix FLOUR, BAKING POWDER, and SALT. Cut in MARGARINE. Combine EGG, MILK, and HONEY; add to dry ingredients and stir until all are just moistened. Using 2 knives, spread on ZUCCHINI mixture and bake at 350° for 25 minutes. Serve slightly warm with cream or whipped cream.

This one is a real puzzler unless you know the secret—is it apple? Is it pear? No one will guess unless you tell.

STEAMED PUDDING

MARGARINE   1 tablespoon, soft
BROWN SUGAR   1/2 cup, firmly packed
EGG   1 whole, beaten
ORANGE EXTRACT   1/2 teaspoon
GROUND CARDAMON   1/2 teaspoon
FLOUR   1-3/4 cups, unsifted
BAKING POWDER   2 teaspoons
SALT   1/4 teaspoon
MILK   1/2 cup
ZUCCHINI   1 cup diced in 1/4-inch cubes

Cream MARGARINE and SUGAR; add EGG and ORANGE EXTRACT; beat well. Mix together dry ingredients; add to creamed mixture alternately with MILK. Stir in ZUCCHINI. Spoon into oiled custard cups or individual steam-pudding molds. Cover; steam 1 hour for large pudding, or 45 minutes for small ones. Serve with orange sauce. Serves 4 to 6.

Orange Sauce

FROZEN ORANGE JUICE   1 cup, undiluted, thawed
CORNSTARCH   1-1/2 tablespoons
LEMON JUICE   1/2 teaspoon
BUTTER or MARGARINE   `1 tablespoon
SALT   pinch

Combine and bring to boil; simmer until thick and clear, stirring often.

HONEY PUDDING

GREEN or GOLDEN ZUCCHINI   2 pounds medium (or
firm flesh of a very
large one)

HONEY   1/4 cup
SALT   1/8 teaspoon
PUMPKIN PIE SPICE   1/2 teaspoon
CINNAMON   1 teaspoon
MILK   1/3 cup
EGG   1 whole
FLOUR   1/3 cup
NUTMEG
SHREDDED COCONUT

Trim ends from ZUCCHINI; steam until tender. Put into blender container
with HONEY, SALT, spices, and MILK. Blend until smooth. Add EGG and
blend. Stir in FLOUR; mix well. Turn into custard cups; sprinkle tops with
NUTMEG and SHREDDED COCONUT. Bake at 300° for 1 hour. Serve
slightly warm or cold with sweetened whipped cream. Serves 4.

MERINGUE ZUCCHINI PIE (or tarts)*

Shell

SUGAR   2 tablespoons
UNSALTED BUTTER   1 cup
SALT   pinch
FLOUR   2 cups
WATER   5 or 6 tablespoons, cold

Mix SUGAR, BUTTER, SALT, and FLOUR until homogenous. Add cold WATER gradually, enough to bind. Do not overwork dough while adding water or it may become rubbery. Roll out pastry; line 2 pie tins or 6 tart pans. Blanch (prebake) shells at 450° until firm, but not browned.

Zucchini Filling

SUGAR   2 pounds
LEMON   1, sliced
VANILLA   1 tablespoon
WATER   2 cups
ZUCCHINI   2-1/2 pounds small

Combine SUGAR, LEMON, VANILLA, and WATER; bring to boil. Wash ZUCCHINI, trim off and discard ends. Slice into 1/2-inch round pieces; put into boiling syrup. Cook until transparent and slightly candied. Drain dry. Save syrup for other usages.

*As served by Chef Francois Kissel at the Brasserie Pittsbourg, Seattle.

Custard Filling

EGG YOLKS   3
SUGAR   5 tablespoons
CORNSTARCH   1 teaspoon
LEMON RIND   1/3 teaspoon grated
VANILLA   1/2 teaspoon
MILK   1 cup, boiling

Mix EGG YOLK, SUGAR, CORNSTARCH, and LEMON RIND. Add VANILLA and boiling MILK. Simmer to thicken. Put aside to cool.

Meringue

EGG WHITES   4
SALT   pinch
VANILLA   1 teaspoon
SUGAR   6 tablespoons

Whip 4 EGG WHITES with pinch of SALT until very stiff. Add VANILLA and SUGAR; mix well.

Garnish

GREEN CANDIED FRUIT or
GREEN CRYSTALLIZED SUGAR   bits of

In precooked pie shells, spread cold custard evenly. Top with well-drained ZUCCHINI. Cover with meringue. Bake at 300° for 15 to 20 minutes until meringue is browned nicely. Garnish with GREEN CANDIED FRUIT or GREEN CRYSTALLIZED SUGAR.

RHUBARB ZUCCHINI PIE

ZUCCHINI   3 cups diced
RHUBARB   1 cup sliced
SUGAR   1-1/4 cups
APPLE PIE SPICES   1-1/2 teaspoons
SALT   pinch
FLOUR   1/4 cup
FROZEN CONCENTRATED APPLE JUICE   1/4 cup,
thawed

EGGS   2 whole, beaten
PASTRY   for 2-crust 9-inch pie
SUGAR   to sprinkle on crust

Combine all ingredients except PASTRY. Pour into unbaked PASTRY shell, cover with top crust and cut slits for steam to escape. Sprinkle lightly with SUGAR. Bake at 400° for 20 minutes, then at 350° until golden brown and done.

ICE CREAM

VANILLA

PLAIN GELATIN   1-1/2 teaspoons
COLD WATER   1/4 cup
ZUCCHINI   1-1/2 cups peeled and diced
HONEY   1/2 cup
VANILLA   1 teaspoon
EVAPORATED CANNED MILK   1 13-ounce can
MILK or CREAM

Soften GELATIN in WATER. Simmer ZUCCHINI in HONEY until tender. Blend well in blender. Add softened GELATIN, VANILLA, and CANNED MILK. Stir well. Add enough MILK to bring mixture up to 22 or 23 ounces. Chill mixture for 3 hours. Pour into Ice Cream Machine and freeze until done.

DATE COCONUT

DATES   1/2 cup chopped
SHREDDED COCONUT   1/4 cup

Make only 21 ounces of Vanilla Ice Cream mixture, then add DATES and COCONUT after 1/2 hour of freezing process.

BUTTER PECAN

PECANS   1/2 cup broken or chopped
BUTTER or MARGARINE   1 tablespoon

Make only 21 ounces of Vanilla Ice Cream mixture. Saute PECANS in BUTTER; cool. Add this to mixture after 1/2 hour of freezing process.

Recipes make 1 quart.

Recipes for use in Salton Ice Cream Machine.

MILK SHAKES

BUTTERSCOTCH

ZUCCHINI   1/2 cup sliced
HONEY   2 tablespoons
BUTTERSCOTCH FLAVORING   2 teaspoons
COLD WATER   2 tablespoons
DRY POWDERED SKIM MILK   3/4 cup
ICE CUBES   crushed

Put all ingredients in blender, except ICE CUBES. Zoom until well blended. Add crushed ICE CUBES, one at a time, with blender on high, until shake is thick. This may take 5 to 7 cubes, depending on ICE CUBE size. Work quickly for a really thick shake. Serve at once.

Chocolate: Same as butterscotch, but use 2 teaspoons CHOCOLATE FLAVORING EXTRACT.

PINEAPPLE

FROZEN CONCENTRATED PINEAPPLE JUICE   1/2
6-ounce can
ZUCCHINI   1/2 cup sliced
DRY POWDERED MILK   3/4 cup
ICE CUBES   crushed

Directions same as for butterscotch.

Recipes serve 2.

Note: Peel zucchini if peeling is tough or if you want to be sneaky!

CASSEROLES

COLORFUL CASSEROLE

CARROTS   *3 cups sliced and chopped*
VEGETABLE BOUILLON   *1 cube*
WATER   *1/2 cup*
ZUCCHINI   *3 cups sliced and diced (can be from very*
            large one)
EGGS   *2 whole*
SEASONED SALT   *1 teaspoon*
THYME   *1/4 teaspoon*
PARSLEY   *1 tablespoon chopped*
FRESH GROUND PEPPER
MILK   *1-1/2 cups*
BREAD CRUMBS *or* CRACKER CRUMBS   *1-1/2 cups*
MEDIUM CHEDDAR CHEESE   *1 cup shredded*

Chop CARROTS with food chopper or whirl in blender to chop coarsely. Dissolve BOUILLON in boiling WATER; add CARROTS; cover and simmer slowly 10 minutes. Add diced ZUCCHINI; simmer a few minutes, stirring occasionally. Drain; add seasonings. Beat EGGS with MILK; add CRUMBS and CHEDDAR CHEESE; stir in vegetables. Turn into greased casserole; bake at 350° for 40 minutes or until set. Serves 6 to 8.

BAKED VEGETABLE RICE

> WATER   1-1/2 cups, boiling
> CHICKEN BOUILLON   1 cube
> SALT   1/2 teaspoon
> BROWN RICE   1/2 cup
> CARROTS   1/2 cup shredded
> ONION   1/2 large, chopped
> CELERY   1 stalk, thinly sliced

Combine in shallow casserole; bake at 350° for 15 minutes.

Then add:

> ZUCCHINI   2 cups thinly sliced
> PARSLEY   1/4 cup chopped
> LEFTOVER VEGETABLES   any cooked ones

Bake 15 minutes longer or until rice has absorbed all liquid.

> EGGS   2 whole
> MILK   1/2 cup
> MEDIUM CHEDDAR CHEESE   1/2 cup grated

Stir EGGS and MILK together and stir into hot rice mixture. Top with CHEDDAR CHEESE. Bake another 30 minutes or until set and browned. Serves 6.

POTATO BAKE

ZUCCHINI   3 cups sliced

VEGETABLE OIL   1 tablespoon

TOMATOES   4, quartered (or 1 16-ounce can tomatoes, drained)

FLOUR   1 tablespoon

ONION SALT   1 teaspoon

FROZEN FRENCH-FRIED POTATOES   1 10-ounce package, thawed

MEDIUM CHEDDAR CHEESE   4 thick slices

Saute ZUCCHINI in OIL for 5 minutes. Add TOMATOES; saute until well heated through. Sprinkle with FLOUR and ONION SALT; spoon into shallow oiled casserole. Cover with thawed POTATOES and bake at 350° for 20 minutes. Top with CHEDDAR CHEESE slices and bake an additional 10 minutes. Serves 4.

CONTINENTAL VEGETABLES

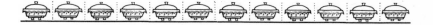

ZUCCHINI   *2 cups sliced*
GREEN PEPPER   *1, diced*
CARROTS   *1 cup shredded*
SHALLOTS   *1/4 cup sliced (or use 1 chopped green onion*
                  plus 1 small clove garlic)
SALT and PEPPER   *to taste*
VEGETABLE OIL   *2 tablespoons*
YOGURT or DAIRY SOUR CREAM   *3/4 cup*
PARMESAN CHEESE   *1/2 cup grated*
PARSLEY   *2 tablespoons chopped*
THYME   *1/2 teaspoon crumbled*
CRUMBS   *2 tablespoons, buttered*
PARMESAN CHEESE   *2 tablespoons*

*In large skillet, saute vegetables in oil for 5 minutes. Season to taste with
SALT and PEPPER. Mix YOGURT or SOUR CREAM with CHEESE,
PARSLEY, and THYME. Stir into vegetables; spoon into buttered
casserole. Sprinkle top with mixed CRUMBS and PARMESAN CHEESE.
Bake at 350° for 30 minutes. Serves 4.*

ZUCCHINI RING

ZUCCHINI   5 cups cubed (can be peeled cubes of very
            large one)
SKIM MILK POWDER   3 tablespoons
WHEAT GERM   4 tablespoons
VEGETABLE OIL or MELTED MARGARINE
                                    2 tablespoons

EGGS   2 whole, beaten
ONION SALT
FRESH GROUND PEPPER

Peel and cube ZUCCHINI; steam until very tender. Drain and mash in
colander, reserving the juice. Measure 1/4 cup of this juice; add SKIM MILK
POWDER, WHEAT GERM, OIL, and beaten EGGS. Beat in mashed
ZUCCHINI. Season with ONION SALT and PEPPER. Bake in small oiled
tube pan at 300° for 45 minutes. Remove from pan to hot platter. Center can
be filled with vegetable of contrasting color, or creamed meat or fish.
Serves 4.

FRIED SPAGHETTI

BACON   4 slices, chopped
EGGS   3 whole
SALT   2 teaspoons
FRESH GROUND PEPPER   1/2 teaspoon
ONION   2 tablespoons grated
MEDIUM CHEDDAR CHEESE   1/2 cup shredded
SPAGHETTI   8 ounces, cooked and drained
ZUCCHINI   1-1/2 cups thinly sliced
BUTTER
PARMESAN CHEESE

Fry BACON in large skillet until browned. Beat together EGGS, SALT, PEPPER, and ONION. Stir in CHEESE, SPAGHETTI, and ZUCCHINI. Scoop BACON up with slotted spoon; mix into spaghetti mixture. Pour mixture into heated skillet with bacon fat; fry until brown. Cut across center; turn both halves; fry until brown. Cut in wedges; spread with BUTTER and sprinkle with PARMESAN CHEESE if desired. Serves 6.

BAKED ZUCCHINI WITH CREAM SAUCE

ZUCCHINI   2 medium, cut in 1/2-inch slices
SALT
WHITE SAUCE   1-1/2 cups medium
PARSLEY   1 tablespoon chopped
CHIVES   1 tablespoon chopped
SOFT BREAD CRUMBS   1 cup
BUTTER   3 tablespoons
BASIL   1/4 teaspoon
OREGANO   1/4 teaspoon
SEASONED SALT   1/2 teaspoon

Steam ZUCCHINI slices until tender crisp; drain. Overlap slices in buttered casserole; SALT lightly. Mix chopped PARSLEY and CHIVES into WHITE SAUCE; spoon over ZUCCHINI. Saute BREAD CRUMBS in BUTTER; mix in herbs and seasoning; sprinkle this topping over sauce. Bake at 350° for 1/2 hour. Serves 6.

ZUCCHINI TOSCA

ZUCCHINI   4 cups peeled and cut up (can be firm flesh of
          large one)
ONION   1 medium, diced
SALT   1/2 teaspoon
PEPPER   1/8 teaspoon
PIMENTO   3 tablespoons chopped
SOFT BREAD CRUMBS   1-1/2 cups
MARGARINE or BUTTER   1/4 cup
CONDENSED CREAM OF MUSHROOM SOUP   1 10-
                    1/2-ounce can

MEDIUM CHEDDAR CHEESE   1/4 cup shredded
CELERY SEED   1 tablespoon

Steam ZUCCHINI and ONION until tender; mash. Add SALT, PEPPER,
and PIMENTO; let drain in colander. Saute CRUMBS in butter. Alternate
layers of ZUCCHINI, MUSHROOM SOUP, and CRUMBS in buttered
casserole or individual dishes. Repeat layers. Cover with CHEDDAR
CHEESE and sprinkle with CELERY SEED. Bake at 350° for 25 minutes
(20 minutes for individual dishes). Serves 6 as side dish.

SWISS ZUCCHINI

BUTTER   3 tablespoons
FLOUR   3 tablespoons
MILK   1 cup, hot
ONION   1 tablespoon grated
SALT   1/4 teaspoon
ZUCCHINI   2 cups shredded (firm flesh of large one)
VEGETABLE OIL   1 tablespoon
EGGS   2 whole, hard boiled and sliced
SALT and PEPPER   to taste
SWISS CHEESE   1 cup shredded
BUTTER   1 tablespoon
SOFT BREAD CRUMBS   3 tablespoons

Melt BUTTER; add FLOUR, stirring until it bubbles. Add hot MILK slowly, stirring constantly until smooth. Add grated ONION and SALT; cook 5 minutes, stirring. Saute shredded ZUCCHINI in OIL slowly for 10 minutes, stirring. Stir in thick cream sauce and sliced EGGS. Add SALT and PEPPER to taste.

Transfer half this mixture to buttered casserole. Top with half of SWISS CHEESE, then add rest of creamed ZUCCHINI. Top with the rest of SWISS CHEESE; sprinkle with buttered CRUMBS. Bake at 400° for 15 minutes, until top is browned and bubbly. Serves 4 to 6.

ZUCCHINI SOUFFLE

ZUCCHINI   3 medium, peeled and sliced
BUTTER   1 tablespoon melted
ONION   2 tablespoons grated
SALT   1 teaspoon
SUGAR   1/8 teaspoon
FRESH GROUND PEPPER
EGGS   3 whole, separated
FRESH SOFT BREAD CRUMBS   1/4 cup

Steam ZUCCHINI until very tender; drain in cheesecloth-lined colander; squeeze out excess juice. Mash and beat until smooth; drain again in colander. Add BUTTER, ONION, SALT, SUGAR, PEPPER, and EGG YOLKS. Mix well and beat. Fold in 3 stiffly-beaten EGG WHITES. Spoon carefully into individual oiled souffle molds. Sprinkle with CRUMBS. Bake at 375° for 25 minutes or until set and puffed. Serve at once. Serves 4.

COMPANY SOUFFLE OMELET

BUTTER   3 tablespoons
FLOUR   4 tablespoons
MILK   1 cup, hot
ONION   1 tablespoon grated
SALT   1/4 teaspoon
EGGS   3 whole, separated
ZUCCHINI   2 cups, any size, peeled and cubed. This makes
        about 1 cup when steamed and mashed.
SALT and PEPPER   to taste
SOFT BREAD CRUMBS   3 tablespoons, buttered

Melt BUTTER; add FLOUR; stir until it bubbles. Add hot MILK slowly, stirring constantly until smooth. Add grated ONION and SALT; cook 5 minutes, stirring. Pour this into beaten EGG YOLKS; mix. Steam ZUCCHINI until tender, about 15 to 20 minutes depending on maturity of squash and size of cubes. Drain in colander; mash; drain again. Add mashed ZUCCHINI to cream sauce, season to taste, and cool. Fold in stiffly-beaten EGG WHITES. Transfer mixture to large buttered iron skillet or casserole. Sprinkle with buttered CRUMBS; bake in preheated 350° oven for 35 to 40 minutes, or until firm and set. Loosen edges; turn out onto hot platter. Serves 4.

EASY OMELET

ZUCCHINI   1 medium, sliced
ONION   1/2 small, chopped
GREEN PEPPER   1/2, chopped
VEGETABLE OIL   2 tablespoons
POTATO   1 small, boiled and diced
EGGS   4 whole
SALT and PEPPER   to taste

Saute ZUCCHINI, ONION, and GREEN PEPPER in OIL until ZUCCHINI is barely tender. Add diced POTATO. Beat EGGS lightly and season; pour over vegetables and cook slowly until firm. Turn out onto hot plate; cut in wedges. Serves 4.

A hearty brunch for Sunday morning.

BAKED OMELET

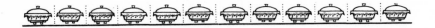

ZUCCHINI   2 cups peeled and cubed (can be firm flesh of
                    very large one)
ONION   1/2, grated
EGGS   5 whole, beaten
MEDIUM CHEDDAR CHEESE   1/2 cup shredded
FRESH GROUND PEPPER
SEASONED SALT   to taste
PARSLEY   1 tablespoon chopped
CRACKER CRUMBS or DRY BREAD CRUMBS
                                                                4 tablespoons

Steam ZUCCHINI cubes until tender; mash and drain in colander. Combine
with rest of ingredients, except CRUMBS. Pour into greased pan; top with
CRUMBS. Bake at 350° for 45 minutes or until completely set. Serves 4.

GOLDEN BROIL

YELLOW or GREEN ZUCCHINI   3 medium
VEGETABLE OIL
MARGARINE   1/4 cup, soft
PARMESAN CHEESE   1/2 cup grated
ONION   1 tablespoon grated
POTATO CHIPS   3 tablespoons crushed
SALT and PEPPER   to taste

Slice ZUCCHINI lengthwise in 1/4-inch-thick slices. Saute each in OIL for several minutes on each side; remove to broiler pan. Combine MARGARINE, CHEESE, ONION, POTATO CHIPS; spread on tops of slices and season to taste. Broil until bubbly and browned. Serves 4 to 6 as side dish.

ZUCCHINI SCALLOP

ZUCCHINI   3 medium, cut in 1/2-inch slices
GARLIC CLOVE   1, crushed
MAYONNAISE   1/2 cup
SOFT BREAD CRUMBS   1/2 cup
MEDIUM CHEDDAR or SWISS CHEESE   1/2 cup grated
CELERY SEED   1/2 teaspoon

Put ZUCCHINI slices in buttered casserole or 9 x 13 x 2-inch pan. Mix crushed GARLIC into MAYONNAISE; spread over ZUCCHINI slices. Bake at 350° for 20 minutes. Combine BREAD CRUMBS and CHEESE; scatter evenly over top; sprinkle with CELERY SEED. Bake at 350° for 20 minutes more or until ZUCCHINI is tender.

Very good as leftovers.

STOVE-TOP CASSEROLE

ZUCCHINI   4 cups sliced (can be from large one, center pulp
                discarded)
VEGETABLE OIL   3 tablespoons
GARLIC CLOVES   2, crushed
SALT and FRESHLY GROUND PEPPER
SPAGHETTI SAUCE   1 16-ounce can, heated
MOZZARELLA CHEESE   3/4 pound, thinly sliced
OREGANO   1 teaspoon crushed
BASIL   1/4 teaspoon

In large Teflon skillet saute ZUCCHINI slices 1 cup at a time, in 1 tablespoon
OIL, with GARLIC. Cook until almost tender and a little brown; drain on
paper towels. Pour off any excess OIL; then layer hot ZUCCHINI in skillet,
seasoning lightly with SALT and PEPPER, and spreading each layer with
some of the hot SPAGHETTI SAUCE and sliced MOZZARELLA
CHEESE. Cover top layer with CHEESE and sprinkle with herbs. Cover
and cook very slowly until mixture is just bubbly and cheese is melted.
Serves 6.

BLENDER CASSEROLE

ZUCCHINI   4 cups sliced (can be thawed slices of frozen
            zucchini)
EGGS   3 whole
SEASONED SALT   1 teaspoon
FRESHLY GROUND PEPPER   1/2 teaspoon
WORCESTERSHIRE SAUCE   1/2 teaspoon
BRAN   1/4 cup
WHEAT GERM   1/4 cup
BUTTERED CRUMBS   1/2 cup
MUSHROOMS   1/2 pound, sliced
ONIONS   1/4 cup finely chopped
CHEDDAR CHEESE   1/2 cup shredded
PAPRIKA

Put ZUCCHINI in blender container with EGGS, SALT, PEPPER, and
WORCESTERSHIRE SAUCE. Blend. Stir in BRAN and WHEAT GERM. Put
1/2 of the BUTTERED CRUMBS in the bottom of a large shallow oiled
casserole. Layer on half of the MUSHROOMS and all of the chopped
ONIONS. Cover with the rest of the ZUCCHINI mixture. Top with CRUMBS
and shredded CHEESE. Sprinkle heavily with PAPRIKA. Bake at 350° for
25 minutes. Check for doneness. If casserole shape is deep instead of
shallow, it may take 30 minutes to bake. These could also be baked in 6
individual ramekins, for festive servings. Takes about 18 to 20 minutes for
these small dishes. Serves 6.

MEDLEY OF VEGETABLES

EGGPLANT   1 medium, peeled and cut in 1/2-inch slices
ZUCCHINI   2 medium, cut in 1/2-inch slices
EGGS   2 whole
BUTTER
CREAM CHEESE   1 3-ounce package
BEER SAUCE
MONTEREY JACK CHEESE   3 large slices
CHEDDAR CHEESE   4 ounces, sliced

Dip EGGPLANT and ZUCCHINI in EGG and saute in BUTTER approximately 5 minutes on each side. Place layer of EGGPLANT in casserole; top with CREAM CHEESE and layer of ZUCCHINI; cover with BEER SAUCE. Continue layering, substituting MONTEREY JACK and CHEDDAR CHEESE (reserve last slice of each) for CREAM CHEESE. Top each layer with BEER SAUCE; then put last slices of MONTEREY JACK and CHEDDAR CHEESES on top. Place uncovered in oven and bake at 350° for 45 to 50 minutes. Makes 6 servings.

Beer Sauce

CONDENSED TOMATO SOUP   1 10-1/2-ounce can
MUSHROOMS   1 3-ounce can, sliced and drained
STEWED TOMATOES   1 14-1/2-ounce can
BEER   1/2 cup
TOMATO PASTE   1 6-ounce can
GREEN PEPPER   1/2, diced
ONION   1 medium, diced
OREGANO   2 teaspoons
BASIL   1/2 teaspoon
SALT   1 teaspoon

Combine all ingredients in saucepan. Bring to a boil and simmer 5 minutes.

QUICK CHEESE CASSEROLE

ZUCCHINI   2 medium, thinly sliced

ONION   1, sliced and separated into rings

TOMATOES   3, sliced (or 1 14-1/2-ounce can tomatoes, drained)

CELERY   1 cup thinly sliced

FROZEN PEAS   1/2 10-ounce package, thawed

ONION SALT   1/8 teaspoon

FRESH GROUND PEPPER   1/4 teaspoon

CONDENSED CHEESE SOUP   1 10-1/2-ounce can

PAPRIKA

Mix vegetables with ONION SALT and PEPPER; put in greased casserole. Bake at 325° for 15 minutes. Spread CHEESE SOUP on top; sprinkle with PAPRIKA. Bake until ZUCCHINI is tender and CHEESE is bubbly. Serves 4.

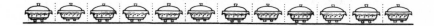

CASSEROLES

with

MEAT

POULTRY

FISH

ZUCCHINI TACOS

VEGETABLE OIL   1 teaspoon
LEAN GROUND BEEF   1/4 pound
ONION   1 small, finely chopped
ZUCCHINI   1 medium, diced
GREEN CHILIES   1/4 cup chopped (optional)
TOMATOES   2, quartered
TACO SAUCE   1 cup
TACO SHELLS
YELLOW CHEESE   grated
LETTUCE   shredded
ONION   sliced

Heat OIL in skillet; add crumbled GROUND BEEF and cook until meat loses its pink color. Drain off fat. Add ONION, ZUCCHINI, GREEN CHILIES, and TOMATOES. Cook slowly until ZUCCHINI is tender. Add TACO SAUCE; reheat. Serve in heated TACO SHELLS garnished with CHEESE, LETTUCE, and ONION. Serves 4.

BETTE'S BELLA ZUCCHINI

ZUCCHINI   1 medium large (8 to 10 inches)
OLIVE OIL   2 tablespoons
GROUND BEEF   1/2 pound
HAM   1/2 cup diced
ONION   1 small, chopped
PARSLEY   2 tablespoons chopped
OREGANO LEAVES   1/2 teaspoon crumbled
SALT and PEPPER   to taste
TOMATO SAUCE   2 tablespoons
FINE BREAD CRUMBS   2/3 cup
BUTTER   2 tablespoons, melted
PARMESAN CHEESE   grated

Split ZUCCHINI lengthwise; scoop out all of center pulp and seeds; chop and put aside. Saute BEEF, HAM, and ONION in OLIVE OIL; add rest of ingredients except BUTTER and CHEESE. Mix in pulp; pile into scooped-out centers; top with BUTTER and PARMESAN CHEESE. Bake at 350° for 1 hour or until tender. Serves 2 to 4.

MOTHER'S CASSEROLE

GROUND BEEF or LAMB   1 pound

ONION   1, chopped

TOMATOES   1 28-ounce can, drain and reserve liquid

GREEN PEPPER   1 small, cut in strips

ZUCCHINI   6 medium, thickly sliced

MEDIUM CHEDDAR CHEESE   3/4 cup shredded

FLOUR   2 tablespoons

RIPE OLIVES   1/2 cup sliced

GARLIC CLOVE   1, crushed

SALT   1 teaspoon

OREGANO   1/4 teaspoon

PARMESAN CHEESE   grated

PAPRIKA

Sprinkle salt in hot Teflon* skillet; add meat and ONION; saute until meat is light brown and crumbly. Drain off extra fat. Add drained TOMATOES, GREEN PEPPER strips, and ZUCCHINI slices; saute 10 minutes. Add reserved TOMATO liquid mixed with 2 tablespoons FLOUR, CHEESE, OLIVES, GARLIC, and seasoning. Reheat for a minute; then spoon into casserole. Sprinkle thickly with the PARMESAN CHEESE and PAPRIKA. Bake at 350° for 1 hour until thick and browned. Serves 6 to 8.

* If not using Teflon, use 1 tablespoon vegetable oil.

BEER BARREL STEW

BEER   2 cups

BEEF STOCK or BEEF BOUILLON   1/2 cup

ONIONS   2 large, sliced

BEEF CHUCK   2 pounds, cut in bite-size pieces

CARROTS   3 large, diced

MUSHROOMS   1/2 cup sliced

CELERY   1 stalk, sliced

ZUCCHINI   2 medium, sliced

TURNIP   1, cubed

SALT and PEPPER   to taste

NUTMEG   pinch

POWDERED LEMON PEEL   1/4 teaspoon

POWDERED BAY LEAF   1/4 teaspoon

MILD CHEDDAR CHEESE   1/2 cup shredded

POTATOES   2 cups mashed, hot

PARSLEY   2 tablespoons chopped

Boil BEER to reduce it to half; add BEEF STOCK. Spread ONIONS in large Dutch oven; cover with layers of BEEF CHUCK and top with layer of vegetables mixed together, sprinkling with SALT and PEPPER. Add NUTMEG, LEMON PEEL, and BAY LEAF to hot BEER liquid; pour over mixture in pot. Cover tightly and bake at 350° for 4 to 4-1/2 hours. Stir CHEESE into mashed POTATOES; spoon around outer edge of hot stew. Broil, uncovered, until POTATOES are lightly browned. Sprinkle with PARSLEY. Serves 6 to 8.

ZUCCHINI WITH MEAT BALLS

ZUCCHINI   1 very large

TOMATOES   1 28-ounce can

TOMATO SAUCE   1 8-ounce can

WORCESTERSHIRE SAUCE   1 teaspoon

GROUND LAMB or BEEF   1 pound

EGG   1 whole

RICE   1 cup cooked

ONION   1/2 cup finely chopped

SALT   1/2 teaspoon

FRESH GROUND PEPPER   1/4 teaspoon

FRESH MINT LEAVES   1 tablespoon chopped (with lamb)

FRESH DILL LEAVES   1 tablespoon chopped (with beef)

Cut ZUCCHINI in quarters lengthwise; scoop out center pulp; put pulp in large skillet with TOMATOES, TOMATO SAUCE, and WORCESTERSHIRE SAUCE. Mix rest of ingredients except ZUCCHINI and form into small meat balls. Heat tomato mixture to simmering; drop in meat balls; simmer slowly for 15 minutes, covered. Slice ZUCCHINI quarters in half lengthwise; cut into thin slices; add to simmering meat balls. Cover and cook slowly until ZUCCHINI is tender. Serves 4.

SWISS STEAK WITH INVISIBLE ZUCCHINI

ROUND STEAK   2 pounds, cut in serving-size pieces
FLOUR   1/2 cup
VEGETABLE OIL   2 tablespoons
SALT and PEPPER   to taste
ZUCCHINI   3 cups peeled and diced (can be firm flesh of
            very large one)
ONION   1, sliced
CELERY   4 stalks, sliced
GREEN PEPPER   1, cut in chunks
TOMATOES   2 cups cooked or canned (optional)

Place *ROUND STEAK* on *floured* cutting board, cover with *FLOUR* and pound it into meat; turn and do the same. Brown pieces in hot *OIL*; season to taste; pour off any excess *OIL*. Turn down heat; put diced *ZUCCHINI* around *STEAK* pieces; cover with sliced vegetables. Cook slowly for 3 hours or until *STEAK* is fork tender. *ZUCCHINI* will provide needed moisture for slow cooking. 2 cups cooked (or canned) *TOMATOES* may be added; any extra juice can be evaporated at end of cooking time by simmering uncovered. Serves 4.

CHARD-STUFFED ZUCCHINI

ZUCCHINI   1 large, cut in half lengthwise
VEGETABLE OIL
SWISS CHARD   2 cups cooked and chopped
GROUND BEEF or LAMB   1 pound
ONION   1, finely chopped
CONDENSED TOMATO SOUP   1/2 10-1/2-ounce can
PEPPER   1/4 teaspoon
THYME   1/2 teaspoon
SALT   3/4 teaspoon
SOFT BREAD   4 slices, cubed
PARSLEY   3 tablespoons chopped
PARMESAN CHEESE   1/4 cup grated
EGGS   2 whole, beaten

Scoop out seeds and pulp from center of ZUCCHINI halves; discard. Score ZUCCHINI flesh in 1-inch squares and rub with OIL. Cook SWISS CHARD until tender; drain well and chop finely.

Stuffing: Sprinkle salt in hot Teflon* skillet; brown meat and ONION. Drain off fat. Add TOMATO SOUP and seasonings; simmer 5 minutes to blend flavors. Stir in rest of ingredients; mix well. Fill centers of ZUCCHINI halves with mixture, pressing into place. Bake in shallow oiled pan or on cookie sheet at 325° for about 1 hour or until ZUCCHINI is tender. Cut in crosswise slices. Serves 8.

* If not using Teflon, add 1 tablespoon vegetable oil.

STUFFED ZUCCHINI FINGERS

ZUCCHINI   12 small (or more)
VEGETABLE OIL   2 tablespoons
MEAT STUFFING (see recipe below)
SAUCE (see recipe below)

Hollow out ZUCCHINI with apple corer (if longer than 3 inches, cut into 3-inch lengths). Stuff with meat mixture; saute in OIL for 10 minutes, turning gently. Place in shallow greased casserole, top with sauce, and bake at 350° for 1/2 hour.

Meat Stuffing

GROUND BEEF or LAMB   3/4 pound
ONION   1, finely chopped
WHEAT GERM   1/4 cup
EGG   1 whole, beaten
SALT and PEPPER   to taste

Saute meat and ONION until meat loses its red color. Cool; add WHEAT GERM, beaten EGG, and seasoning; mix.

Sauce

CORNSTARCH   2 teaspoons
YOGURT   1 pint
GARLIC SALT   1/2 teaspoon
OREGANO   1/2 teaspoon, if using beef
MINT   1/2 teaspoon, crushed, if using lamb

Mix CORNSTARCH with half of YOGURT; stir into the other half and add seasonings. Heat on low until piping hot; pour over ZUCCHINI fingers and bake.

ZUCCHINI A LA MADDALENA

ZUCCHINI   3 large
GROUND BEEF   1 pound
BREAD CRUMBS   1/2 cup
PARMESAN CHEESE   1/4 cup grated
EGG   1 whole
SALT and PEPPER   to taste
PARSLEY
VEGETABLE OIL
TOMATO SAUCE   1 8-ounce can

Parboil ZUCCHINI. Split lengthwise into 4 parts; remove pulp; squeeze out excess water. Add pulp to GROUND BEEF, BREAD CRUMBS, CHEESE, and EGG; add SALT, PEPPER, and PARSLEY to taste; mix well.

Sprinkle ZUCCHINI shells with SALT and place in baking dish that is at least 1 inch deep. Brush shells lightly with OIL; fill with meat mixture. Dilute TOMATO SAUCE with 1/2 can of water and pour over and around ZUCCHINI. Bake at 350° for 1 hour. While baking, baste ZUCCHINI with drippings. Make sure pan always has at least 1/2-inch liquid around shells, adding more water if necessary.

NOODLE CASSEROLE

GROUND BEEF   1 pound
TOMATO SAUCE   2 8-ounce cans
OREGANO   1/2 teaspoon
ZUCCHINI   3 cups sliced
SALT
WIDE NOODLES   8 ounces
COTTAGE CHEESE   1 cup
CREAM CHEESE   4 ounces, softened
FRESH GROUND PEPPER   1/8 teaspoon
GREEN ONIONS   4, finely chopped
YOGURT or DAIRY SOUR CREAM   1/4 cup

Cook BEEF in skillet until meat loses its red color; drain off fat. Add
OREGANO, TOMATO SAUCE, and ZUCCHINI. Simmer 5 minutes; add
SALT to taste. In the meantime, cook NOODLES in salted water until
tender; drain. Put half of NOODLES in shallow greased baking dish. Mix 1
teaspoon SALT, COTTAGE CHEESE, CREAM CHEESE, PEPPER,
GREEN ONIONS, and YOGURT or SOUR CREAM. Spread this on
NOODLES; add remaining NOODLES. Pour meat-ZUCCHINI mixture
over top. Bake in moderate oven (350°) about 30 minutes. Serves 6.

Good also when reheated.

POTATO POT

ZUCCHINI   3 cups sliced

ONION   1/4 cup minced

MARGARINE   1/4 cup

ROAST BEEF, LAMB, or PORK   2 cups diced

POTATOES   6 medium, cooked and diced

MILK   1/2 cup

DRY RED WINE   1/2 cup

SOY SAUCE   2 tablespoons

PARSLEY   2 tablespoons chopped

THYME   1/4 teaspoon

MARJORAM   1/4 teaspoon

SALT and PEPPER   to taste

PAPRIKA   1/2 teaspoon

Saute ZUCCHINI and ONION in MARGARINE for 2 to 3 minutes. Add remaining ingredients, except PAPRIKA; mix well. Put in large casserole and sprinkle with PAPRIKA. Bake at 350° for 45 minutes, basting occasionally with liquid of casserole. When cooked, thicken if necessary. To thicken pour off 1/4 cup liquid; cool in saucepan and mix in 1 tablespoon flour. Pour off rest of hot liquid into saucepan; simmer, stirring until thickened and smooth. Pour back over casserole. Serves 6.

No roast? Try spam or other canned pressed meat.

GOULASH

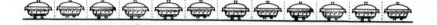

ELBOW MACARONI   8 ounces
GROUND BEEF   1 pound
ONION   1, chopped
ZUCCHINI   3 cups sliced
FROZEN PEAS   1/2 10-ounce package, thawed
TOMATOES   1 7-1/2-ounce can. Drain and reserve liquid
FLOUR   1 tablespoon
SALT   2 teaspoons
FRESH GROUND PEPPER   1/2 teaspoon
CONDENSED TOMATO SOUP   1 10-1/2-ounce can
SOFT BREAD CRUMBS   1/2 cup
MARGARINE   2 tablespoons, melted

Cook and drain MACARONI. Cook BEEF and ONION in hot salted Teflon skillet until meat loses its red color. Drain off fat. Add ZUCCHINI slices, thawed PEAS, and TOMATOES; saute 5 minutes, stirring gently. Add TOMATO liquid mixed with FLOUR, cooked MACARONI, seasonings, and TOMATO SOUP. Mix well and heat through. Pour into 2-quart shallow casserole. Mix BREAD CRUMBS with melted MARGARINE; sprinkle on top of mixture. Bake at 350° approximately 26 minutes. Serves 6 to 8.

DANISH ZUCCHINI GOULASH

BEEF STEW MEAT   *1 pound, cubed*
VEGETABLE OIL   *1 tablespoon*
SALT   *2 teaspoons*
FRESH GROUND PEPPER   *1/2 teaspoon*
GROUND BAY LEAVES   *1/2 teaspoon*
ZUCCHINI   *5 cups peeled and cubed (can be from very large one)*
ONION   *1, coarsely chopped*
FROZEN APPLE JUICE   *1/4 cup, thawed but not diluted*
FLOUR   *1 tablespoon*
PAPRIKA   *1 tablespoon*
VINEGAR   *1 tablespoon*
FROZEN APPLE JUICE   *2 tablespoons, undiluted*
DAIRY SOUR CREAM   *1/2 cup*
NOODLES   *4 cups cooked and buttered*

Brown BEEF cubes in hot OIL; add seasonings, 3 cups ZUCCHINI, ONION, and APPLE JUICE. Simmer slowly, covered, for 2 to 3 hours or until meat is very tender. Cubed ZUCCHINI will cook up and form thick juice around meat. 15 minutes before serving, mix in remaining ZUCCHINI; cook 5 minutes, covered. Mix FLOUR and PAPRIKA with VINEGAR and APPLE JUICE; stir this into cooking meat sauce. Stir and simmer 10 minutes until ZUCCHINI is barely tender and sauce well thickened. Stir in SOUR CREAM just before serving. Good on buttered NOODLES. Serves 4 to 6.

MEAT LOAF

ZUCCHINI   2 medium, chopped (or 3 cups large chopped
            zucchini)
ONIONS   2 small, chopped
TOMATOES   2, chopped (or 1 7-1/2-ounce can tomatoes,
            drained)
VEGETABLE OIL   1 tablespoon
EGG   1 whole
WORCESTERSHIRE SAUCE   1 tablespoon
GARLIC CLOVE   1, crushed
SALT   1 teaspoon
FRESH GROUND PEPPER   1/2 teaspoon
SAGE   1/2 teaspoon
SOFT BREAD CRUMBS   1/2 cup
GROUND BEEF   1-1/2 pounds

Saute ZUCCHINI, ONIONS, and TOMATOES in OIL; simmer until
tender. Cool, drain, and mash. Beat EGG; stir in WORCESTERSHIRE
SAUCE, GARLIC, seasonings, and mashed vegetables. Add BREAD
CRUMBS and GROUND BEEF; mix well. Let stand at room temperature
for 1/2 hour; then pack into oiled loaf pan, mound up top, and bake at 325°
for 1-1/2 hours. Drain off accumulated fat. Let stand at room temperature for
15 minutes before slicing. Serves 8.

MOUSSAKA CASSEROLE

GROUND LAMB or BEEF   1 pound

ONIONS   2, chopped

TOMATOES   4, chopped (or 1 14-1/2-ounce can tomatoes, drained)

RED WINE   1/4 cup

FRESH GROUND PEPPER   1/8 teaspoon

CINNAMON   1/8 teaspoon

PARSLEY   3 tablespoons chopped

THYME   pinch

SALT   to taste

EGGPLANT   1 medium, peeled and cut in 1/2-inch-thick slices

ZUCCHINI   2 medium, cut in 1/2-inch-thick slices

VEGETABLE OIL

COTTAGE CHEESE   1 cup, drained (or dry curd)

WHITE SAUCE   1-1/2 cups, medium-thick

SOFT BREAD CRUMBS   1/2 cup

PARMESAN CHEESE   3/4 cup grated

Heat large Teflon skillet; sprinkle with salt; add meat and ONIONS; stir fry until meat starts to brown. Add TOMATOES, WINE, PEPPER, CINNAMON, PARSLEY, and THYME. Simmer until thick and liquid has cooked out, stirring occasionally. Add SALT to taste. Saute EGGPLANT and ZUCCHINI slices in OIL until almost tender. Add COTTAGE CHEESE to WHITE SAUCE. In buttered 9 x 13-inch pan or large casserole, layer the EGGPLANT on the bottom. Combine BREAD CRUMBS and PARMESAN; sprinkle half of it on the EGGPLANT; top with half of meat mixture. On top of this layer ZUCCHINI slices; sprinkle with rest of BREAD CRUMBS and PARMESAN, and rest of meat mixture. Top with WHITE SAUCE mixture. Bake at 350° for 1 hour or until bubbly and browned. Let casserole stand for 15 minutes or more before serving. Serves 6.

SPAGHETTI SAUCE

SALT   1/2 teaspoon

GROUND BEEF   1/2 pound

MUSHROOMS   1/2 pound, sliced (or 1 4-ounce can mushroom stems and pieces)

GREEN PEPPER   1, chopped

TOMATOES   2, quartered

GARLIC CLOVE   1, minced (or 1/2 chopped ONION)

RED WINE   1/2 cup

CONDENSED TOMATO SOUP   1 10-1/2-ounce can

OREGANO   1/2 teaspoon

THYME   pinch

BASIL   pinch

SUGAR   1/4 teaspoon

ZUCCHINI   2 medium, cut in half lengthwise, then cut crosswise in thin slices

SALT and PEPPER   to taste

Saute GROUND BEEF in hot salted Teflon skillet until lightly browned; pour off most of fat. Add MUSHROOMS, GREEN PEPPER, TOMATOES, and GARLIC or ONION, and saute a few minutes longer. Add WINE, TOMATO SOUP, herbs, and SUGAR; stir. Simmer 1/2 hour to blend flavors. Add thin ZUCCHINI slices; simmer until ZUCCHINI is tender. SALT and PEPPER as necessary. This makes a nice thick sauce. Serves 4.

ZUCCHINI LASAGNA

ONION   1/2 cup finely chopped

GARLIC   1 clove, minced

OLIVE OIL   2 tablespoons

GROUND BEEF   1 pound

TOMATO SAUCE   1 8-ounce can

TOMATO PASTE   1 6-ounce can

WATER   3/4 cup

MUSHROOMS   1 2-ounce can, sliced

ITALIAN SEASONING   3/4 teaspoon

SALT   2 teaspoons

EGG   1 whole, beaten

ZUCCHINI   2 cups grated

COTTAGE CHEESE   2 cups

PARMESAN CHEESE   1/4 cup grated

LASAGNA NOODLES   1 8-ounce package

MOZZARELLA CHEESE   1/2 pound, sliced

Saute ONION and GARLIC in OIL. Add GROUND BEEF and cook until brown. Add TOMATO SAUCE, TOMATO PASTE, WATER, MUSHROOMS with liquid, ITALIAN SEASONING, and 1 teaspoon SALT. Simmer uncovered 15 to 20 minutes.

Combine beaten EGG, ZUCCHINI, COTTAGE CHEESE, PARMESAN CHEESE, and remaining 1 teaspoon SALT.

Cook LASAGNA in boiling salted water until tender (about 10 minutes). Place in colander under running cold water and drain on paper towels.

Pour 1/2 of the meat sauce in bottom of 9 × 13-inch pan. Cover with layer of LASAGNA (6 noodles, overlapping), 1/2 the ZUCCHINI mixture, another layer of NOODLES, 1/2 the CHEESE slices, the rest of the ZUCCHINI mixture, final layer of NOODLES, the rest of the meat mixture, and top with CHEESE.

Cover and bake at 375° for 30 minutes. Uncover and bake 10 minutes more. Makes 8 to 10 servings.

Reprinted from the Seattle Post-Intelligencer by permission of Louis Guzzo.

ECCEDENZA DILETTO ("leftover delight")

WATER   2 cups
OIL or BUTTER   1 teaspoon
CHICKEN SEASONED STOCK BASE   2 teaspoons
RICE   1 cup raw
BUTTER or MARGARINE   4 tablespoons
ZUCCHINI   3 small, thinly sliced
ONION   1 cup chopped
WHOLE KERNEL CORN   1 8-ounce can, drained (or leftover fresh corn cut from the cob)
TOMATOES   1 1-pound can, cut in quarters
SALT   1-1/2 teaspoons
PEPPER   1/4 teaspoon
GROUND CORIANDER SEED   1 teaspoon
LEAF OREGANO   1 teaspoon
LEFTOVER LAMB ROAST   3 to 4 cups cooked, cut in cubes
LEFTOVER VEGETABLES   if desired
TOMATO SAUCE   1 8-ounce can
BUTTER or MARGARINE   4 tablespoons
CURRY POWDER   3/4 teaspoon
BREAD   3 slices, cubed or crumbled

Put WATER in saucepan. Add OIL and CHICKEN STOCK BASE. Bring to a boil, stir in RICE and cook according to package directions. Melt BUTTER in skillet and saute ONION and ZUCCHINI until almost tender.

Pour RICE in a large greased casserole. Add ZUCCHINI and ONION. Add CORN, TOMATOES and juice, SALT, PEPPER, CORIANDER, OREGANO, meat, and LEFTOVER VEGETABLES, if desired. Add enough TOMATO SAUCE to moisten.

Melt BUTTER in skillet. Stir in CURRY. Add BREAD cubes and mix well. Sprinkle over top of casserole. Bake at 350° for 20 to 25 minutes or until heated through. Serves 8 to 10.

Recipe by Ruth deRosa, reprinted from the Seattle Times.

SLOW COOKERY
PORK CHOPS AND ZUCCHINI

ZUCCHINI   3 small, cut in 1/4-inch slices
PORK CHOPS   4
FRESH GROUND PEPPER
GARLIC POWDER
CHICKEN BOUILLON CUBE   1
HOT WATER   3 tablespoons
BASIL   1/4 teaspoon
OREGANO   1/4 teaspoon
FLOUR   to thicken juice, if desired
COOKED RICE

Slice ZUCCHINI into bottom of slow cookery pot. Trim fat from PORK CHOPS. Rub hot frying pan with trimmed pork fat; discard fat. Brown the PORK CHOPS on both sides in frying pan. Season with PEPPER and GARLIC POWDER. Drain off any excess fat. Transfer PORK CHOPS to slow cooker. Dissolve BOUILLON in WATER, pour over PORK CHOPS and ZUCCHINI. Sprinkle with herbs. Cook 1/2 hour on high, then turn to low and cook 6 to 8 hours. Juice can be thickened with FLOUR, to serve on RICE.

BIG CIRCLES

ZUCCHINI   4 1-1/2-inch-thick slices from very large one
BROWN RICE   1 cup freshly cooked
MEDIUM CHEDDAR CHEESE   1/3 cup grated
HAM, CHICKEN, or LEFTOVER MEAT   1/2 cup minced
SEASONED SALT   1/2 teaspoon
RED WINE   1/4 cup
FRESH GROUND PEPPER
PAPRIKA
RED WINE   1/4 cup, for basting

Cut across ZUCCHINI in 1-1/2-inch slices; do not peel. Remove center pulp and seeds; discard, leaving large rings for stuffing. Put these on greased baking sheet or in shallow pan. Combine all ingredients except PAPRIKA; fill centers of rings. Sprinkle generously with PAPRIKA. Bake at 350° for 35 minutes or until ZUCCHINI is tender, basting twice. Serves 4.

REFRESHING OVEN STEW

FROZEN MIXED VEGETABLES   1 10-ounce package
POTATO   1 small, peeled and cubed
WATER   1/4 cup
VEGETABLE BOUILLON CUBE   1
WORCESTERSHIRE SAUCE   1 teaspoon
SOY SAUCE   2 tablespoons
TOMATOES   2, quartered
CAULIFLOWER or BROCCOLI FLOWERETS   1 cup
ZUCCHINI   2 medium, sliced
ONION   1 small, chopped
LEFTOVER MEAT   1 cup cubed (or 1/2 cup slivered lunch
                 meat)
SEASONED SALT   1 teaspoon
OREGANO   1/4 teaspoon
SAGE   pinch

In Dutch oven with lid, simmer FROZEN MIXED VEGETABLES and
POTATO cubes for 5 minutes in WATER with BOUILLON,
WORCESTERSHIRE, and SOY SAUCE added. Add rest of vegetables,
meat, and seasonings. Cover and bake at 350° for 40 minutes or until
vegetables are tender. Juice can be poured off and thickened for thicker stew.
Serves 4.

Stew can be cooked on top of stove, but cook very slowly, covered; stir occasionally,
checking to be sure it does not cook dry.

HAM LUNCH

MARGARINE   *2 tablespoons, soft*
BUTTER FLAVORING   *1/4 teaspoon*
ZUCCHINI   *3 cups sliced*
MUSHROOMS   *1/2 pound, sliced*
GREEN ONIONS   *2 cups thinly sliced*
PRESSED HAM LUNCHEON MEAT   *1 5-ounce package, slivered*
SEASONED SALT   *1/2 teaspoon*
FRESHLY GROUND PEPPER   *1/4 teaspoon*
ROMANO CHEESE   *grated, to garnish*

Add BUTTER FLAVORING to MARGARINE in fry pan or wok. Saute ZUCCHINI, MUSHROOMS, and GREEN ONIONS until barely tender. Stir in HAM and seasonings; saute until HAM is heated through. Serve garnished with CHEESE. Serves 3 or 4.

ZUCCHINI TETRAZZINI

ZUCCHINI   3 cups diced (can be firm flesh of very large one)
SALT
HAM   2 cups cooked, cut in strips
MUSHROOMS   1/2 pound, sliced
MARGARINE   1/4 cup, soft
ONION   1 small, diced
FLOUR   1/4 cup
CHICKEN BOUILLON   1 cup, hot
MILK   1 cup
SWISS CHEESE   1/3 cup shredded
DRY MUSTARD   1/2 teaspoon
FRESH GROUND PEPPER   1/8 teaspoon
PARMESAN CHEESE   1/3 cup grated
SLIVERED ALMONDS   optional

Steam ZUCCHINI until barely tender; SALT lightly; drain and keep warm.
In large saucepan, saute HAM and MUSHROOMS in MARGARINE
about 3 minutes; remove and keep warm. Saute ONIONS until golden, then
blend in FLOUR. Gradually add BOUILLON and MILK; cook over low
heat, stirring, until thick and smooth. Add SWISS CHEESE, MUSTARD,
and PEPPER; stir until CHEESE melts. Add HAM and MUSHROOMS;
stir in drained ZUCCHINI. Spoon into shallow buttered casserole; sprinkle
with PARMESAN CHEESE and scatter ALMONDS on top. Broil until
light brown and bubbly. Serves 6.

MACARONI CON ZUCCHINI

ELBOW MACARONI   1 8-ounce package

ONION   1 large, chopped

VEGETABLE OIL   1 tablespoon

ZUCCHINI   2-1/2 cups diced (can be from large one)

MUSHROOMS   1/4 pound, sliced

RIPE OLIVES   1/4 cup sliced

MARGARINE   2 tablespoons

FRENCH DRESSING   1/4 cup

MEDIUM PROCESS CHEESE   1/4 cup shredded

PARMESAN CHEESE   1/4 cup grated

MILK   3 tablespoons

PASTRAMI   1/4 pound sliced, cut in strips

OREGANO   1/4 teaspoon crushed

FRESH GROUND PEPPER   1/8 teaspoon

SALT   to taste

PAPRIKA

Boil *MACARONI* in salted water until tender; drain. Saute *ONION* in *OIL;* stir into *MACARONI*. Saute rest of vegetables in *MARGARINE* and *FRENCH DRESSING* until *ZUCCHINI* is barely tender. Add to *MACARONI* with cheeses, *MILK*, *PASTRAMI*, and seasonings. Mix; turn into shallow casserole. Sprinkle with *PAPRIKA*; bake at 350° for 20 minutes. Serves 6.

Very good reheated.

ITALIAN SKILLET

HOT ITALIAN SAUSAGES   2
ZUCCHINI   4 medium, sliced
ONION   1, coarsely chopped
TOMATO SAUCE   1 8-ounce can
OREGANO   1/2 teaspoon
GARLIC SALT   1/2 teaspoon
SUGAR   1/2 teaspoon
BASIL   1/2 teaspoon
FRESH GROUND PEPPER   1/4 teaspoon
WHEAT GERM   2 tablespoons

Slice SAUSAGE very thin; saute in Teflon* skillet for 10 minutes; set aside.
Saute ZUCCHINI and ONION in same skillet for 5 minutes or until ONION
is golden. Add TOMATO SAUCE and seasonings; sprinkle with WHEAT
GERM. Arrange SAUSAGE slices on top of mixture; cover and cook for 10
minutes. Serves 4.

* If not using Teflon, add bit of vegetable oil, then drain off oil after all sauteing.

CORNMEAL CASSEROLE

YELLOW CORNMEAL   1 cup
SALT   1 teaspoon
FRESH GROUND PEPPER   1/8 teaspoon
ONION   1/2, grated
WATER   2-3/4 cups
HOT ITALIAN SAUSAGES   2, thinly sliced
MUSHROOMS   1/2 pound, sliced
ZUCCHINI   2-1/2 cups sliced
RIPE OLIVES   1/2 cup sliced
WATER   1 cup
RED WINE   1/2 cup
TOMATO PASTE   1 6-ounce can
DRY SPAGHETTI SAUCE SEASONING MIX   1 package
PARMESAN CHEESE

Mix *CORNMEAL, SALT, PEPPER,* and *ONION* with 1 cup cold *WATER.* Stir this into 1-3/4 cups boiling *WATER.* Cook, stirring, until mixture boils; then cook on very low heat for 10 minutes. Pour into buttered 8 x 8-inch pan and chill several hours or overnight. Cut cornmeal into 1-inch squares.

Saute thinly-sliced *SAUSAGE* in skillet until browned; pour off excess fat. Add *MUSHROOMS* and *ZUCCHINI;* saute a few minutes more. Add *OLIVES, WATER, WINE, TOMATO PASTE,* and *SPAGHETTI SEASONING MIX.* Simmer 10 minutes. Arrange cornmeal cubes in shallow buttered 2-quart casserole. Cover them with *ZUCCHINI* sauce. Sprinkle with *PARMESAN CHEESE;* bake at 350° for 25 to 30 minutes. Serves 6.

This is good hot, cold, or reheated.

BACON ZUCCHINI DINNER

BACON   1 pound, sliced
ONION   1-1/4 cups chopped
GREEN PEPPER   3/4 cup
GARLIC CLOVE   1, crushed
ZUCCHINI   3 cups sliced
RIPE OLIVES   1 cup sliced
SHERRY or RED WINE   1/4 cup
FLOUR   1 tablespoon
CONDENSED TOMATO SOUP   1 10-1/2-ounce can
SALT   1/4 teaspoon
CHILI POWDER   1 teaspoon
ROMANO CHEESE   1/4 cup grated

Cook BACON in skillet until crisp. Drain on paper towel. Pour off most of fat; add chopped ONION, GREEN PEPPER, and GARLIC. Saute 3 minutes; add ZUCCHINI; saute 5 minutes, stirring gently. Stir in half the BACON. Add OLIVES, SHERRY mixed with FLOUR, TOMATO SOUP, and seasonings. Heat through; spoon into oiled casserole. Sprinkle with ROMANO CHEESE; bake at 350° approximately 20 minutes. Garnish with remaining half of BACON. Serves 6 to 8.

On a tight budget? Make this with 1/2 pound bacon and skip the garnish. It still tastes delicious.

ZUCCHINI QUICHE

PIE SHELL   9-inch, unbaked

MARGARINE   1 tablespoon, soft

BACON   8 slices

ZUCCHINI   3 cups cubed (can be firm flesh of large one,
         peeled and center pulp discarded)

EGGS   4 whole

CREAM or UNDILUTED CANNED MILK   1/2 cup

MARJORAM   1/2 teaspoon

BASIL   1/2 teaspoon

ONION SALT   3/4 teaspoon

CAYENNE PEPPER   dash

SWISS or MEDIUM CHEDDAR CHEESE   (or combination)
         2 cups shredded

Spread PIE SHELL with soft MARGARINE, sprinkle with BACON that has been fried crisp, drained on absorbent paper, and crumbled.

Steam ZUCCHINI until tender, then drain well. Combine ZUCCHINI with EGGS in blender container and blend until smooth. Add CREAM; blend briefly to mix. Stir in seasonings and fold in CHEESE. Pour into the prepared PIE SHELL. Bake at 425° for 10 minutes, then reduce heat to 300° and bake for 30 to 40 minutes, or until center is set, and a knife inserted halfway between edge and center comes out clean. Let stand 10 minutes before cutting to serve. Serves 6.

Note: These can be made in little foil pie tins for individual servings. In individual pielets, bake at 375° for about 30 to 35 minutes.

EASY WIENER BAKE

WIENERS   1 pound, thinly sliced
CELERY   1 cup thinly sliced
ONION   1, chopped
ZUCCHINI   3 cups cubed (can be firm flesh of very large one)
VEGETABLE OIL   2 tablespoons
FROZEN PEAS   1 10-ounce package, thawed
CONDENSED CREAM OF MUSHROOM SOUP   1 10-
1/2-ounce can
POTATO CHIPS   2 cups crushed

In large Teflon skillet saute WIENERS, CELERY, ONION, and ZUCCHINI for 5 minutes in OIL. Add PEAS and MUSHROOM SOUP; heat. Spoon into shallow greased casserole. Top with crushed POTATO CHIPS. Bake at 350° for 40 minutes. Serves 6.

CHICKEN WITH HERBS

WHEAT GERM   2 tablespoons

FLOUR   2 tablespoons

CHICKEN SEASONED SALT   1 teaspoon

FRYER THIGHS   8 (or chicken pieces)

VEGETABLE OIL   2 tablespoons

TOMATO SOUP   1 10-3/4-ounce can

TOMATOES   6, cut in wedges

ZUCCHINI   2 cups sliced

SEASONED SALT   1 teaspoon, or less, to taste

THYME   1 teaspoon

BASIL   1/2 teaspoon

IMO or YOGURT   1/2 cup

NOODLES   hot buttered

Combine WHEAT GERM, FLOUR, and CHICKEN SEASONED SALT. Toss CHICKEN parts in this to coat well. Heat OIL in large skillet and brown CHICKEN. Add TOMATO SOUP; cover and cook on very low heat for 45 minutes, stirring occasionally. Add TOMATOES, ZUCCHINI, and seasonings. Cover and simmer 15 minutes more, until vegetables are tender. Remove vegetables and CHICKEN to hot serving dish. Stir IMO into sauce in skillet. Reheat, but do not boil. Serve on hot buttered NOODLES. Serves 4.

MRS. PITRE'S
CHICKEN-SMOTHERED ZUCCHINI

FRYER   1 small, cut up

SALT and PEPPER   to taste

VEGETABLE OIL   2 tablespoons

ZUCCHINI   2 medium

CHICKEN LIVER

BUTTER   1 tablespoon

GARLIC SALT   pinch

FRESH TARRAGON   1 teaspoon chopped

RICE   2 cups cooked and buttered

Cut up FRYER; set LIVER aside. Season FRYER to taste; brown in OIL in Dutch oven. Cover and cook very slowly for 35 minutes. Slice ZUCCHINI; add to CHICKEN. Cover again and cook slowly for 10 minutes, stirring carefully from time to time. Saute chopped CHICKEN LIVER in BUTTER; sprinkle it with GARLIC SALT. Add to CHICKEN; stir gently. Sprinkle with chopped TARRAGON. Serve on hot buttered RICE. Serves 4.

EASY COMBO

HAM   3 slices, cooked and cut in narrow strips
CHICKEN LIVERS   1/2 pound, cut up
MUSHROOMS   1/4 pound, sliced
BUTTER or MARGARINE   3 tablespoons
CONDENSED TOMATO SOUP   1 10-1/2-ounce can
SHERRY or RED WINE   3 tablespoons
ZUCCHINI   3 cups steamed cubes
ROMANO CHEESE   1/4 cup grated

Saute HAM, LIVERS, and MUSHROOMS in BUTTER. Add TOMATO SOUP and SHERRY; heat but do not boil. Steam ZUCCHINI cubes until tender; add to mixture and stir lightly. Sprinkle with grated ROMANO CHEESE; brown lightly under broiler. Serves 4 to 6.

QUICK ORIENTAL DINNER

Shrimp Stir-Fry

ZUCCHINI   2 cups cut in matchlike strips
CELERY   1 cup cut in diagonal slices
GREEN PEPPER   1, cut in strips
MUSHROOMS   1/2 pound, sliced
VEGETABLE OIL   1 tablespoon
SHRIMP   1 4-1/2-ounce can, drained
JERUSALEM ARTICHOKES*   ("sunchokes") 1 cup peeled
                                            and sliced

In a large skillet or wok, saute ZUCCHINI, CELERY, GREEN PEPPER, and MUSHROOMS in OIL, stir-frying for 5 minutes. Add SHRIMP and ARTICHOKES; cover and steam 3 to 5 minutes.

Egg Foo Yung

EGGS   3 whole
ONION   1 small, grated
BEAN SPROUTS   1/2 cup
ZUCCHINI   1 cup unpeeled and grated, drained in colander

This is about the only vegetable I know of that grows more easily than zucchini.

WHEAT GERM   1/2 cup
SALT   1/2 teaspoon
VEGETABLE OIL
RICE   cooked

Beat EGGS until thick and lemon colored. Stir in rest of ingredients except
OIL and RICE. Drop from tablespoon onto hot, oiled griddle. Brown on
one side; turn and brown other side. Serve with Sweet and Sour Sauce and
fluffy RICE.

Sweet and Sour Sauce

FROZEN APPLE JUICE   1/4 cup, undiluted
CATSUP   1 tablespoon
CORNSTARCH   2 teaspoons
SOY SAUCE   1 tablespoon
VINEGAR   1/4 cup

Heat APPLE JUICE and CATSUP together. Dissolve CORNSTARCH in
SOY SAUCE and VINEGAR; add to APPLE JUICE. Simmer until thick
and clear.

TUNA BOATS

TUNA   2 6-1/2-ounce cans, drained
OLIVES   1 cup chopped
SOFT BREAD CRUMBS   1-1/2 cups
GARLIC CLOVES   2, crushed
PARSLEY   2 tablespoons chopped
GREEN PEPPER   1. finely chopped
EGGS   2 whole, beaten
ZUCCHINI   6 medium, cut in half lengthwise
VEGETABLE OIL
WHITE WINE

Drain. TUNA and flake. Add chopped OLIVES, BREAD CRUMBS, GARLIC, PARSLEY, GREEN PEPPER, and beaten EGGS. Steam or boil ZUCCHINI for 5 minutes; scoop out the center pulp and seeds and discard, leaving only 1/4-inch-thick shell for stuffing. Replace pulp with tuna stuffing, mounded up. Arrange ZUCCHINI halves on greased cookie sheet or shallow baking pan. Bake at 350° for about 30 minutes until ZUCCHINI is tender, basting occasionally with mixture of equal amounts of OIL and WHITE WINE. Serves 6.

PICKLES

RELISHES

WATERMELON PICKLES

ZUCCHINI   3 pounds, peeled
ALUM   4 tablespoons
WATER   3 quarts
ICE CUBES

Syrup

SUGAR   8 cups
CINNAMON STICKS   4
VINEGAR   4 cups
CLOVES   4 teaspoons
SUGAR   1-1/2 cups

Peel and chunk ZUCCHINI. Heat ALUM in 3 quarts water but do not boil. Pour this over ZUCCHINI; cover with ICE CUBES and let stand 2 hours. Drain. Bring syrup ingredients to boil; pour over ZUCCHINI and leave overnight. Drain and reheat this syrup 3 mornings, adding an additional 1/2 cup SUGAR each time, and pour over ZUCCHINI. Red or green food coloring may be added. Boil up, pack into sterilized jars, and seal on the third day.

BREAD AND BUTTER PICKLES

ZUCCHINI   *4 quarts chunks or small slices*
WHITE ONIONS   *6, sliced*
GREEN PEPPERS   *2, chopped*
RED PEPPERS   *2, chopped*
GARLIC CLOVES   *2*
PICKLING SALT   *1/2 cup*
CRACKED ICE

Syrup

SUGAR   *5 cups*
CIDER VINEGAR   *3 cups*
TURMERIC POWDER   *1-1/2 teaspoons*
MUSTARD SEED   *2 tablespoons*
CELERY SEED   *1 teaspoon*

Put everything but ICE and syrup in crock. Put cracked ICE over top. Let stand 3 hours. Drain, but do not wash. Bring syrup ingredients to boil; add pickle ingredients; cook about 20 minutes. Pack into sterilized jars and seal.

DILL PICKLES

DILL HEADS   6
GARLIC CLOVES   6
HORSERADISH ROOT   6 thin slices
ZUCCHINI   5 pounds, cut in chunks (can be firm flesh of
              very large one)
WATER   2 quarts
VINEGAR   1 quart
SALT   2/3 cup
ALUM   1 teaspoon

Put 1 HEAD DILL, 1 CLOVE GARLIC, 1 slice HORSERADISH ROOT
in each pint jar. Wash and pack ZUCCHINI chunks into jars. Boil up
WATER and VINEGAR; add SALT and ALUM; pour over ZUCCHINI
chunks in jars and seal. Process in water bath for 5 minutes. These are ready
to eat in 6 weeks. Makes approximately 6 pints.

SANDWICH PICKLES

ZUCCHINI   2 pounds small
ONIONS   2 small, peeled and sliced
WATER
SALT   1/4 cup
WHITE VINEGAR   2 cups
PICKLING SPICES   3 teaspoons
TURMERIC POWDER   1 teaspoon
SUGAR   2 cups

Slice ZUCCHINI and ONIONS; cover with WATER and add SALT. Let stand 3 hours. Drain. Combine remaining ingredients; bring to boil. Pour over slices and let stand for 2 hours; then bring syrup and slices to a boil for 5 minutes. Pack in sterilized jars and seal hot.

CHRISTMAS RELISH

ZUCCHINI   12 cups coarsely ground
GREEN PEPPERS   2, coarsely ground
SWEET RED PEPPERS   2, chopped
ONIONS   4 cups coarsely ground
PICKLING SALT   1/3 cup
TURMERIC POWDER   1 teaspoon
CURRY POWDER   1 teaspoon
CELERY SEED   1 teaspoon
CORNSTARCH   1 tablespoon
PEPPER   1/2 teaspoon
VINEGAR   3 cups
SUGAR   4-1/2 cups

In large enamel pan, mix PICKLING SALT into vegetables. Let stand overnight. Drain and rinse with cold water. Mix together rest of ingredients; add to vegetables in large enamel pan; boil 20 minutes. Pour into sterilized jars and seal.

ZUCCHINI JUICE

Peel, remove, and discard seedy pulp from a very large zucchini. Cut in pieces and feed into vegetable juicer. The pale green liquid that comes out (in profusion) can be used in many ways to add taste and nutrition in cooking — any place where water would ordinarily be used. It can be stored for several days in refrigerator or frozen.

For convenience, freeze juice in ice cube trays. When solidly frozen, remove cubes from trays, and store in plastic bag in freezer. Remove one or two at a time as needed; they melt easily for use in cooking.

Suggested uses: As "water" for cooking other vegetables or for making soups, in gravies or cream sauces, as liquid in Jello for vegetable salad.

ZUCCHINI RELISH

CELERY   4 stalks, chopped
ZUCCHINI   10 cups peeled and chopped (can be firm flesh of
            very large one)
ONIONS   4 large, chopped
RED PEPPER   1, chopped
PICKLING SALT   1/2 cup
VINEGAR   3 cups
SUGAR   3-1/4 cups
CELERY SEED   2-1/2 teaspoons
MUSTARD SEED   2-1/2 teaspoons
TURMERIC POWDER   2 teaspoons
CORNSTARCH   2 tablespoons, dissolved in
VINEGAR   1/2 cup

Combine vegetables and PICKLING SALT in large enamel or stainless steel pan; let stand overnight; then drain and rinse well. Bring to boil VINEGAR, SUGAR, and seasonings; add chopped vegetables; remove from heat and let stand for 2 hours. Return to stove; bring to boil. Add CORNSTARCH dissolved in VINEGAR; simmer 15 minutes. Spoon into sterilized jars; seal. Process in water bath for 20 minutes. Makes about 15 half-pints.

ZUCCHINI FISH SAUCE (Tartar Sauce)

ZUCCHINI   1/2 cup shredded, drained (can be firm flesh of
            very large one)
DAIRY SOUR CREAM   3/4 cup
MAYONNAISE   1/4 cup
PREPARED HORSERADISH   1 tablespoon
DILL PICKLE   1 tablespoon finely chopped
CHIVES   1 tablespoon finely chopped
SALT   1/4 teaspoon
WHITE PEPPERCORNS   1/8 teaspoon fresh ground

Mix all together; chill. Serve like tartar sauce with fish.

SYLVIA'S ZUCCHINI MARMALADE

ORANGE   1, seeded
MARASCHINO CHERRIES and SYRUP   1 8-ounce jar
YELLOW or GREEN ZUCCHINI   5 pounds seeded and
                peeled (can be from very large ones)
CRUSHED PINEAPPLE and JUICE   1 20-ounce can
LEMONS   juice of 2
SUGAR   5 pounds

Slice ORANGE and peeling; chop in blender (or grind). Put in large cooking
kettle. Chop CHERRIES in blender (or grind); add to kettle. Chop
ZUCCHINI in blender — 2-1/2 pounds coarsely chopped, 2-1/2 pounds
blended quite fine; add all to cooking kettle. Add rest of ingredients; mix
together and cook until desired thickness is obtained. Pour into sterilized jars
and seal.

LOW-SODIUM CHUTNEY

ZUCCHINI   *6 cups sliced and ground coarsely (use very large zucchini, remove center pulp and seeds, but do not peel)*

GREEN PEPPERS   *2, coarsely ground*

TART APPLES   *2 cups, cored but not peeled, coarsely ground*

ONION   *1, finely ground*

RAISINS or DATES   *3/4 pound, ground*

CELERY SEED   *1 tablespoon*

HONEY   *1 cup*

LEMON   *1, juice and grated rind*

VINEGAR   *1-1/3 cups*

FROZEN CONCENTRATED ORANGE JUICE   *1/3 cup, undiluted*

Combine all ingredients and simmer until thick. Spoon into sterilized jars; seal and process in boiling water bath for 10 minutes. Jars to be used soon need not be processed; keep well in refrigerator. This chutney mellows and blends flavors after a week or two.

Note: *This really spices up a no-salt diet. Of your garden vegetables, zucchini is lowest in sodium, .06 milligrams per 1/2 cup zucchini.*

LAVERNE'S QUICK CHUTNEY

BUTTER or MARGARINE   1/4 cup

TURMERIC   1 teaspoon

CINNAMON STICKS   2

POWDERED CORIANDER   1 teaspoon

SALT   1/2 teaspoon (optional)

MUSTARD SEED   1 teaspoon

ZUCCHINI   2 cups cut into 1/2-inch cubes

BROWN SUGAR   1 cup packed

LEMON   1, quartered and thinly sliced

TOMATOES   1 15-ounce can, drained

CRUSHED PINEAPPLE   1 8-ounce can, drained

CHUNK PINEAPPLE   1 20-ounce can, drained

VINEGAR   1 scant cup

Melt BUTTER in heavy frying pan and add seasonings. Saute ZUCCHINI, add BROWN SUGAR and LEMON and cook 2 or 3 minutes, stirring. Add TOMATOES, CRUSHED and CHUNK PINEAPPLE, and VINEGAR. Simmer 5 to 10 minutes, stirring often. Remove CINNAMON STICK. Serve hot, or chill in refrigerator. Lasts a long time in the refrigerator.

SOUPS

SALADS

SALAD DRESSING

VEGETABLE SOUP

SOUP MEAT (NECK)   1-1/2 pounds
SOUP BONES   1/2 pound, cracked
ONION   1, chopped
POWDERED BAY LEAVES   1/2 teaspoon
FRESH GROUND PEPPER   1/4 teaspoon
CLOVES   pinch
CELERY LEAVES   1/2 cup chopped
WATER   3 quarts cold
ZUCCHINI   3 cups diced—2 cups peeled, 1 cup unpeeled
ONIONS   1 cup sliced
CARROTS   1 cup diced
CELERY   1 cup chopped
POTATOES   1 cup diced
TOMATOES   1 28-ounce can
SOUP MIX GRAINS   1/4 cup
SALT and PEPPER   to taste

Trim fat off SOUP MEAT; cut in 3/4-inch cubes. Put SOUP MEAT, BONES, ONION, seasoning, and WATER in large soup pot. Bring to boil; lower heat and simmer 4 hours, covered. Remove SOUP BONE; skim off fat. Add vegetables and cook 35 to 45 minutes. Season to taste. Serves 6 to 8.

CREAM OF ZUCCHINI SOUP

WATER   2 cups boiling

CHICKEN BOUILLON CUBES   3

ZUCCHINI   2 cups sliced (can be firm flesh of large one; peel
       if peeling is tough)

WHOLE or SKIM MILK   1 cup

SALT and PEPPER   to taste

PARSLEY   1 tablespoon minced

DAIRY SOUR CREAM   4 teaspoons

Dissolve BOUILLON CUBES in boiling WATER; add ZUCCHINI and cook until tender. Whirl in blender until smooth; return to heat. Add MILK and season to taste. Heat, but do not boil. Serve hot, sprinkled with chopped PARSLEY and teaspoon of SOUR CREAM. Serves 4.

Note: This can be made in winter, with frozen zucchini slices. They need not be blanched to prepare for freezing, if only to be used in this soup recipe. Just slice into plastic bags, close tops securely, label, and put in freezer. Use later when zucchini is out of season.

TOMATOES STUFFED WITH ZUCCHINI

ZUCCHINI   2 cups shredded (can be firm flesh of very large
            one)
SALT   1 teaspoon
TOMATOES   4 large
SALT   1/4 teaspoon
SUGAR   1/8 teaspoon
FRESH GROUND PEPPER   1/8 teaspoon
GARLIC CLOVE   1, crushed
MUSHROOMS   1/2 cup sliced
VEGETABLE OIL   1 tablespoon
MAYONNAISE   4 teaspoons
FRESH PARSLEY   1 tablespoon minced

Slice off top half inch of TOMATOES. Scoop out pulp; chop it and the tops
of TOMATOES; put in colander to drain. Shred ZUCCHINI and sprinkle
with teaspoon SALT; mix with TOMATO pulp; leave to drain for 1/2 hour.
Sprinkle inside of TOMATO shells with mixture of SALT, SUGAR, and
PEPPER. Drain them upside down on paper towels in refrigerator for 1/2
hour or more. Squeeze ZUCCHINI lightly; then saute in Teflon skillet with
TOMATO pulp, GARLIC, MUSHROOMS, and OIL for 5 minutes. Turn
up heat and stir constantly until all moisture is evaporated. Season to taste
with SALT and PEPPER. Cool mixture; chill for 1/2 hour or more. Stuff
TOMATO shells and garnish with MAYONNAISE and PARSLEY.
Serves 4.

TWO-TONE ZUCCHINI GELATIN

PLAIN GELATIN   1 tablespoon
COLD WATER   1/2 cup
ZUCCHINI   1-1/4 cups cubed (unpeeled if small; peeled and
            pulp removed, if large one)
FROZEN CONCENTRATED APPLE JUICE   1/2 cup,
                                        thawed
GREEN FOOD COLORING   2 drops
FROZEN CONCENTRATED APPLE JUICE   1/2 cup

Soak GELATIN in WATER. Simmer ZUCCHINI in 1/2 cup apple juice until tender. Blend in blender. Add FOOD COLORING. Add soaked GELATIN; blend well. Add FROZEN APPLE JUICE; blend. Add more WATER, if necessary, to bring total amount to just under 2 cups. Pour into individual molds or serving glasses. Chill. This forms 2 layers, one solid dark green, one fluffy pale green. Very pretty.

POTATO ZUCCHINI SALAD

SALAD OIL   1/4 cup

POTATOES   3 cups cooked and shredded (do not overcook)

ZUCCHINI   1 cup shredded

ONION   1/2, grated

GARLIC POWDER   1/4 teaspoon

DILL SEED   1/2 teaspoon

SEASONED SALT   1 teaspoon

MAYONNAISE   1/4 cup

FRENCH DRESSING   1/4 cup

Pour OIL over POTATOES, add ZUCCHINI and ONION. Toss lightly. Mix rest of ingredients, stir carefully into POTATO mixture. Chill at least 2 hours before serving. Serves 4.

BEAN ZUCCHINI SALAD

ZUCCHINI   1-1/2 cups small, thinly sliced
GREEN PEPPER   1, cut in strips
GREEN BEANS   1 cup cooked (canned or fresh)
RED KIDNEY BEANS   1 15-1/2 ounce can, drained well
GREEN ONIONS   3, thinly sliced (or 1 medium ONION,
                sliced and separated into rings)
VINEGAR   3 tablespoons
VEGETABLE OIL   3 tablespoons
SEASONED SALT   1 teaspoon
SUGAR   1 teaspoon
FRESHLY GROUND PEPPER   1/4 teaspoon

Combine vegetables. Combine rest of ingredients; pour over vegetables and stir well. Refrigerate in covered bowl for several hours, stirring occasionally. Toss lightly before serving. Serves 6.

SUMMER SUPPER SALAD

MAYONNAISE   1/4 cup

FRENCH DRESSING   1/4 cup

WIENERS   4, cut in half crosswise, then cut in strips

PEAS   1/2 cup cooked

ZUCCHINI   1 cup diced

DILL PICKLE   1/4 cup chopped

CELERY   1/4 cup thinly sliced

CARROT   1/4 cup shredded

SALAD GREENS

Mix together MAYONNAISE and FRENCH DRESSING; add rest of ingredients. Mix lightly; chill well. Serve on SALAD GREENS. Serves 4.

CELERY ZUCCHINI SALAD

ZUCCHINI   1 medium
CELERY   3 stalks
GARLIC SALT   1 teaspoon
WATER   ice
PLAIN YOGURT   1 cup
FRESH GROUND WHITE PEPPER   1/8 teaspoon
ONION SALT   1/2 teaspoon
SALAD HERBS   1/4 teaspoon
SALAD GREENS

Slice ZUCCHINI and CELERY very thin; sprinkle with GARLIC SALT; cover with ice WATER for 1 hour. Drain in colander and pat dry with paper towels. Mix remaining ingredients; toss lightly with CELERY and ZUCCHINI. Serve on SALAD GREENS. Serves 4 to 6.

ZUCCHINI DILL SALAD

Halve several small ZUCCHINI, lengthwise. Scoop out center seeds and pulp. Slice thinly, sprinkle with salt, and drain in colander for 1/2 hour. Pat slices dry with paper towel. For each 2 cups of ZUCCHINI slices, combine dressing of:

> YOGURT   1/2 cup
>
> DAIRY SOUR CREAM   1/4 cup
>
> FRESH DILL LEAVES   2 tablespoons minced
>
> LEMON JUICE   1 tablespoon
>
> TARRAGON LEAVES   1 teaspoon crushed
>
> SHALLOTS   3, finely minced (or 1 small garlic clove, crushed)
>
> SALT and PEPPER   to taste

Stir dressing into ZUCCHINI slices; chill for several hours.

> LETTUCE
>
> TOMATOES

Serve on sliced TOMATOES and LETTUCE leaves. Serves 2 to 4.

TUNA VEGETABLE SALAD

ZUCCHINI   2 cups small sliced (or small slices of very large
            one)
WATER-PACK TUNA   1 7-ounce can, drained
GREEN PEPPER   1/2 cup chopped
CELERY   1/2 cup thinly sliced
ONION   1/2 cup sliced in rings
CHERRY TOMATOES   1 cup halves
MAYONNAISE   1/4 cup
FRENCH DRESSING   1/4 cup
SALAD HERBS   1/4 teaspoon

Steam ZUCCHINI slices 5 minutes; drain on paper towels; chill. Combine
TUNA with rest of vegetables; add MAYONNAISE, FRENCH DRESS-
ING, and SALAD HERBS, stirred together. Mix. Add chilled ZUCCHINI
slices; toss lightly. Chill well. Serves 6.

ITALIAN SALAD

SALAD MACARONI   1/2 12-ounce package
ONION   1, chopped
CELERY   2 stalks, chopped
GARLIC CLOVE   1, crushed
DAIRY SOUR CREAM   1 cup
ZUCCHINI   1-1/2 cups, chopped
PEAS   1/2 cup cooked
CELERY   1/2 cup thinly sliced
RIPE OLIVES   1/4 cup sliced
RADISHES   1/4 cup thinly sliced
ITALIAN HERB SEASONING   1/2 teaspoon
FRENCH DRESSING   3 tablespoons (optional)

Cook *MACARONI* until tender, but not soft, in well-salted water with *ONION, CELERY,* and *GARLIC.* Drain. Add remainder of ingredients; mix well; chill. Just before serving, stir in 3 tablespoons *FRENCH DRESSING* (optional). Serves 8.

APPLE ZUCCHINI SALAD

ZUCCHINI   1 small, thinly sliced
APPLES   2, cored and diced
CELERY   1/2 cup chopped
POTATOES   1 cup cooked, peeled, and cubed
BOTTLED ITALIAN DRESSING   2 tablespoons
TOMATO   1/2 small, peeled, seeded, and cubed
MAYONNAISE   1/4 cup
RED ONION   1 small, thinly sliced into rings
ROMAINE LETTUCE

Marinate ZUCCHINI, APPLE, CELERY, and POTATOES in ITALIAN DRESSING about 1 hour in refrigerator. Stir TOMATO into MAYONNAISE. Toss marinated mixture and half of ONION RINGS with tomato mayonnaise. Serve on ROMAINE and garnish with remaining ONION RINGS. Serves 6.

SALAD DRESSING

ZUCCHINI   *1 medium, peeled and sliced*
CHIVES   *1/4 cup cut up*
GREEN PEPPER   *1/2, cut up*
TOMATO   *1 large, peeled and sliced*
SEASONED SALT   *1 teaspoon*
PARSLEY   *1 tablespoon chopped*
CUCUMBER   *1 small, peeled and sliced*
SALAD HERBS   *1/2 teaspoon*
FRESH GROUND PEPPER   *1/4 teaspoon*
SALAD OIL   *2 tablespoons*
LEMON JUICE   *1 tablespoon*
VINEGAR   *1 tablespoon*

Mix all together in large blender container. Cover and whirl by turning on high speed for a few seconds, switching off several times, until ingredients are well chopped. Makes over 2 cups.

VEGETABLES

SIDE DISHES

STUFFINGS

CREAMY SAUCE

CELERY   2 stalks, thinly sliced
GOLDEN ZUCCHINI   1 cup sliced
GREEN ZUCCHINI   1 cup sliced (or 2 cups green only)
MILK   1/4 cup
CREAM CHEESE   1 3-ounce package, softened and cubed
FLOUR   1 tablespoon
SALT and PEPPER   to taste
SOFT BREAD CRUMBS   3 tablespoons, sauteed in
BUTTER   1 tablespoon

Steam CELERY for 5 minutes; add ZUCCHINI slices and steam until ZUCCHINI is barely tender. In the meantime, put MILK, CREAM CHEESE, and FLOUR in blender; whirl until smooth. Combine with vegetables in Teflon saucepan. Cook over low heat, stirring gently, until sauce thickens and boils. Season to taste. Serve topped with buttered CRUMBS. Serves 4 as side dish.

Note: If you raise your own zucchini, try some of the new hybrid, Golden zucchini, from Burpees. Not much different in taste, but a wonderful very bright yellow color which adds a different look when combined with regular color zucchini.

ZUCCHINI A LA DI JULIO

BACON   2 strips, cut in 1-inch pieces
ZUCCHINI   3 small, about 1 inch in diameter
ONION   1/2 medium
STEWED TOMATOES or TOMATO SAUCE

3 tablespoons
SALT and PEPPER   to taste

Saute BACON until lightly browned; drain excess fat. Cut ZUCCHINI into
1/4-inch slices; slice ONION; mix with ZUCCHINI and add to BACON. Add
TOMATOES, SALT and PEPPER to taste. Cover skillet and steam for 20
minutes or until done.

ZUCCHINI IN AGRODOLCE

ZUCCHINI   6 large, trimmed and cut into quarters
            lengthwise
OLIVE OIL   2-1/2 tablespoons
GARLIC CLOVE   1, crushed
WINE VINEGAR   2-1/2 tablespoons
WATER   2-1/2 tablespoons
PINE NUTS   2 to 3 tablespoons
SEEDLESS WHITE RAISINS   2 to 3 tablespoons
SALTED ANCHOVIES (ITALIAN)   2, chopped
SALT

Prepare ZUCCHINI. Heat OIL in large skillet; saute GARLIC and discard.
Add ZUCCHINI; cover pan and cook a few minutes. Add VINEGAR and
WATER; cook over moderate heat 10 minutes. Add NUTS, RAISINS, and
washed and chopped ANCHOVIES. SALT to taste. Cook 2 to 3 minutes
longer.

QUICK AND SAUCY

VEGETABLE OIL   *1 tablespoon*
ONION   *1, finely chopped*
GARLIC CLOVE   *1, crushed or minced*
ZUCCHINI   *2 medium, cut in 1/4-inch slices*
SALT   *1/4 teaspoon*
FRESH GROUND PEPPER   *1/8 teaspoon*
DRIED MARJORAM   *1/4 teaspoon*
TOMATO SAUCE   *1 8-ounce can*
EGG   *1 whole, hard-boiled, chopped*
PARSLEY   *1 tablespoon chopped*
ONION SALT   *1/4 teaspoon*

Saute ONION and GARLIC in OIL until ONION is golden. Add ZUCCHINI slices and seasoning; saute a few minutes longer. Cover with TOMATO SAUCE and simmer slowly until ZUCCHINI is barely tender. Serve garnished with mixture of EGG, PARSLEY, and ONION SALT. Serves 4.

SUMMER FAVORITE

WATER   1/2 cup

CHICKEN BOUILLON   1 cube

ONION   1 small, sliced and separated into rings

TOMATOES   2 large or 3 small, quartered

FROZEN PEAS   1/2 10-ounce package, thawed (or 1 cup
fresh)

ZUCCHINI   2 cups sliced

FLOUR   1 tablespoon

BASIL   pinch

SEASONED SALT

Dissolve BOUILLON cube in boiling WATER; add ONION, TOMATOES, and PEAS. Cover; simmer gently 5 minutes. Add ZUCCHINI; simmer until ZUCCHINI is barely tender. Remove vegetables from liquid with slotted spoon; keep warm. Pour off 1/4 cup of liquid, cool in measuring cup, and blend in 1 tablespoon FLOUR; return to saucepan with hot liquid; simmer until thickened. Season to taste; add vegetables and reheat. Serves 4.

ORANGE ZUCCHINI

ZUCCHINI   4 cups sliced
SALT
MARGARINE or BUTTER   1 tablespoon melted
MANDARIN ORANGE SECTIONS   1 11-ounce can
CORNSTARCH   2 teaspoons
NUTMEG   1/4 teaspoon
SLIVERED ALMONDS   4 tablespoons

Steam ZUCCHINI slices until barely tender. Remove to pan and SALT lightly. Add melted MARGARINE; set aside and keep warm. Pour syrup from ORANGE sections; blend CORNSTARCH into syrup and simmer until thickened and clear. Add NUTMEG. Add ORANGE sections and reheat. Pour over warm ZUCCHINI slices and sprinkle with SLIVERED ALMONDS. Serves 4 to 6.

CHINESE ZUCCHINI

VEGETABLE OIL   1 teaspoon
CELERY   1 cup thinly sliced
POD PEAS   1/2 pound
MUSHROOMS   1/2 cup sliced
ZUCCHINI   2 cups thinly sliced
BEAN SPROUTS   1/2 pound
SOY SAUCE

In Teflon skillet or wok, cook CELERY in OIL over medium heat, stirring, for several minutes. Add POD PEAS, MUSHROOMS, and ZUCCHINI. Cook, stirring, for several minutes. Add BEAN SPROUTS; stir and cook until BEAN SPROUTS are very lightly cooked. Serve with SOY SAUCE. Serves 4 to 6.

JIFFY SWEET AND SOUR

ZUCCHINI   4 small, sliced
FROZEN APPLE JUICE   1/8 cup, undiluted
CIDER VINEGAR   1/8 cup
GARLIC CLOVE   1, crushed
DILL WEED   1/2 teaspoon

Combine ingredients. Simmer 5 minutes or until ZUCCHINI is barely tender, stirring occasionally. Serves 4.

ZUCCHINI UNO MOMENTO

ZUCCHINI   2 cups sliced
VEGETABLE OIL   1 tablespoon
MUSHROOMS   1 4-ounce can sliced (or stems and pieces)
FLOUR   1-1/2 tablespoons
RED WINE   1/2 cup
OREGANO   1/4 teaspoon
THYME   1/4 teaspoon
SALT   to taste
PARSLEY   1 teaspoon chopped

Saute ZUCCHINI in OIL until barely tender. While it is cooking, prepare sauce. Drain MUSHROOMS; reserve liquid. Blend FLOUR with MUSHROOM liquid. Cook in small saucepan with WINE until thickened, stirring constantly. Add seasonings, then MUSHROOMS and ZUCCHINI. Simmer for a few minutes to blend flavors. Sprinkle with PARSLEY. Serves 4.

CHICKEN-FRIED ZUCCHINI

ZUCCHINI   1 medium
MILK   1-1/2 cups (can be canned milk, even sour canned milk,
    skim or buttermilk)
VEGETABLE OIL   1/4 cup
CORNMEAL   1/2 cup
FLOUR   1/2 cup
SEASONING SALT   1 teaspoon

Slice ZUCCHINI in 5/8-inch rounds; soak in MILK for 1/2 hour or more. Heat OIL in Teflon skillet on medium heat. Lift ZUCCHINI slices out of MILK; dip both sides of each slice in breading mixture of CORNMEAL, FLOUR, and SEASONING SALT (chicken type seasoning is great in this). Place slices in hot OIL and fry until golden; turn and repeat. Do not over-cook. Serves 2.

Note: *If you have no cornmeal, use cornmeal muffin mix instead of the cornmeal and flour mixture, with added seasoning. Save the milk used for soaking to use in gravies and cream sauces.*

ZUCCHINI FRITTERS

ZUCCHINI   4 7-1/2-inch, peeled
SOUR FRENCH BREAD   12 slices
MILK
GARLIC CLOVES   4 medium, pressed
THYME   2 teaspoons
SALT   1-1/2 teaspoons
PEPPER   1/2 teaspoon
PARMESAN CHEESE   2 cups grated
EGGS   3 whole, beaten
FINE BREAD CRUMBS   1-1/2 to 2 cups
OLIVE OIL

Cut ZUCCHINI in half; boil in water until tender. Drain and immediately place in bowl to save exuding juices. When cool, place ZUCCHINI in suitable pan and mash thoroughly. Pour vegetable juices over 1 or 2 slices BREAD, squeeze as dry as possible, and crumble BREAD into mashed ZUCCHINI; continue with vegetable juices until juices are used up, then use small amounts of MILK to finish soaking and crumbling rest of BREAD slices.

Add rest of ingredients except BREAD CRUMBS; mix thoroughly and slowly add CRUMBS, mixing well until consistency is suitable for dropping into fry pan for cooking. (Use only sufficient crumbs to achieve a delicate mixture.) Drop by rounded tablespoons into moderately hot fry pan with OLIVE OIL; flatten to about 2/3-inch thickness, brown on both sides and serve.

ZUCCHINI A LA STELLA

ZUCCHINI   1 pound, cut into 1-inch slices
TOMATO SAUCE   1 8-ounce can
ONION   1, sliced
GREEN PEPPER   1/4 cup chopped
GROUND NUTMEG   1/4 teaspoon
SUGAR   1/4 teaspoon
BAY LEAF   1 crumbled
SALT   1/2 teaspoon
PEPPER   1/2 teaspoon

Mix ingredients in skillet. Simmer until tender, about 20 minutes. Serves 4.

COOKOUT ZUCCHINI—SKEWERED

ZUCCHINI   2 medium
MUSHROOMS   1/2 pound
GREEN PEPPER   1, cut in wedges
CHERRY TOMATOES   1 basket
MARGARINE   melted
HOT BARBECUE SAUCE
SALT and PEPPER   to taste

Slice ZUCCHINI in 1/2-inch rounds; thread on skewers alternating with MUSHROOMS, GREEN PEPPER, and TOMATOES, being careful to skewer ZUCCHINI slices horizontally to keep them firmly in place. Brush with MARGARINE and place on barbecue grill over medium hot coals. Turn occasionally, basting with sauce, for about 15 to 20 minutes. Serves 4 to 6.

COOKOUT ZUCCHINI—IN FOIL

TOMATOES   4, sliced
ZUCCHINI   2 medium, sliced
ONIONS   2 large, thinly sliced
CHICKEN BOUILLON   1 cube per packet
FRESH GROUND PEPPER

Layer several slices of TOMATO, ZUCCHINI, and ONION in center of heavy aluminum foil squares. Sprinkle each packet with one crushed BOUILLON cube and PEPPER. Fold each foil packet and seal with double folds. Place on barbecue grill over medium hot coals; cook 35 to 40 minutes. Serves 6 to 8.

BRAISED PEAS AND ZUCCHINI

ZUCCHINI   2 medium, diced (or 3 to 4 cups diced from large
            zucchini)
FROZEN PEAS   1 10-ounce package, thawed
MARGARINE   2 tablespoons
CHICKEN BOUILLON   1 cube, dissolved in
WATER   2 tablespoons hot
SALT and PEPPER   to taste
CHIVES   1 teaspoon chopped
PARSLEY   1 teaspoon chopped

In large Teflon* skillet, saute ZUCCHINI and PEAS in MARGARINE for 5 minutes. Add BOUILLON cube and WATER; season as necessary. Cover tightly and cook 3 to 5 minutes until vegetables are barely tender. Stir in CHIVES and PARSLEY. Serves 6.

*If not using Teflon, stir often so as not to scorch.

ZUCCHINI WITH PEPPERS

BUTTER or MARGARINE   1 tablespoon
STALE BREAD   2 slices, cubed
SWEET RED PEPPER   1, cut in strips
GREEN PEPPER   1, cut in strips
CELERY   1/2 cup thinly sliced
ONION   1 small, chopped
VEGETABLE OIL   1/4 cup
ZUCCHINI   3 cups sliced
GARLIC SALT   1 teaspoon
FRESH GROUND PEPPER   1/4 teaspoon
PARMESAN CHEESE   1/4 cup grated
MEDIUM CHEDDAR CHEESE   1/4 cup shredded

Melt BUTTER in heavy Dutch oven; stir in STALE BREAD cubes and saute a few minutes. Remove BREAD and set aside. Add RED and GREEN PEPPERS, CELERY, ONION, and OIL; saute until ONION is golden. Add sliced ZUCCHINI, GARLIC SALT, and PEPPER. Cover; cook very slowly for 15 minutes or until ZUCCHINI is tender, stirring occasionally. Sprinkle BREAD cubes over vegetables. Combine PARMESAN and CHEDDAR CHEESES; sprinkle on top; then put uncovered under broiler until BREAD cubes are browned and CHEESE is melted. Serves 4 to 6.

RATATOUILLE

EGGPLANT   1, peeled and cubed

OLIVE OIL   2 tablespoons

GARLIC CLOVES   3, crushed

VEGETABLE OIL   1/2 cup

ZUCCHINI   3 cups sliced (can be from very large one)

ONIONS   3, sliced

GREEN PEPPERS   2, cut in strips

TOMATOES   5, peeled and chopped

CELERY   2 stalks, sliced

PARSLEY   2 tablespoons minced

SALT   1 teaspoon, or to taste

FRESH GROUND PEPPER

THYME   1/2 teaspoon crushed

MARJORAM   1/4 teaspoon

In heavy skillet saute EGGPLANT in OLIVE OIL until light brown. Put
EGGPLANT with GARLIC in large pot or Dutch oven. Add some of
VEGETABLE OIL to skillet; saute ZUCCHINI; remove to pot. Repeat this
with ONION, GREEN PEPPERS, TOMATOES, and CELERY, adding a
little more OIL for each vegetable. Add seasonings to pot and cook mixture,
stirring, for about 10 minutes; then turn heat very low, cover pot, and simmer
slowly for about an hour. If there is any liquid left in pot, uncover and cook it
down. This is delicious hot or cold, a good accompaniment for roasts or as
filling for omelets. Serves 6 to 8.

This mixture freezes very well. Make it in big batches in late summer when these
vegetables are plentiful. Add left-over meats to this for an easy main dish.

QUICK AND CRUNCHY

BACON   4 slices
STALE BREAD   3 slices, cubed
ONION   1 medium, finely chopped
ZUCCHINI   4 cups sliced
VINEGAR   2 tablespoons
FROZEN APPLE JUICE   2 tablespoons, undiluted
SEASONED SALT   1 teaspoon

In skillet, cook BACON crisp; remove and keep warm. Pour off and reserve all but 2 tablespoons of the BACON fat. Toast BREAD, cube, and saute BREAD cubes in this fat until brown; remove and keep cubes hot. Return 2 tablespoons of reserved fat to skillet. Saute ONIONS and ZUCCHINI, stirring gently, until ZUCCHINI is barely tender-crisp. Add VINEGAR, APPLE JUICE, and SALT. Simmer a few minutes, stirring occasionally. Crumble hot BACON; add BACON and BREAD cubes to ZUCCHINI, stir in, and serve at once. Serves 4 to 6.

EASY SKILLET ZUCCHINI

CARROTS   2, thinly sliced
VEGETABLE OIL   3 tablespoons
ONION   2 cups sliced in rings
ZUCCHINI   2 medium, thinly sliced
SALT and PEPPER   to taste
GARLIC POWDER

Saute CARROTS in OIL for 10 minutes. Add ONION rings and ZUCCHINI slices; season with SALT, PEPPER, and GARLIC POWDER. Saute very slowly about 10 minutes, until tender. Serves 4 as side dish.

JIFFY ZUCCHINI IN CHEESE SAUCE

ZUCCHINI   3 cups cubed (can be solid flesh from very large
            one)
MILK   1 cup
CORNSTARCH   1 tablespoon
SEASONING SALT   1 teaspoon
DRY MUSTARD   1/3 teaspoon
COOKING SHERRY or RED WINE   3 tablespoons
GOOD MELTING CHEESE   3 ounces

Cook ZUCCHINI in 1/2 cup MILK in Teflon pan until barely tender.
Remove with slotted spoon and keep warm. Stir CORNSTARCH in 1/2 cup
cold MILK; add to hot MILK in saucepan with SEASONING SALT,
MUSTARD, and WINE. Cook, stirring constantly, until thickened. Add
ZUCCHINI; heat, but do not boil. Add CHEESE, cut in chunks, and stir
only until it melts. Serve at once. Serves 4.

GREEN ZUCCHINI

ZUCCHINI   2 cups cubed (can be firm flesh of very large one)
ITALIAN SALAD DRESSING   1/2 cup
PARSLEY   1 small bunch
GARLIC CLOVE   1, crushed
SOFT BREAD CRUMBS   1/4 cup
DILL PICKLE   1/2, sliced

Simmer ZUCCHINI cubes in ITALIAN DRESSING until barely tender.
Drain dressing off into blender container; add remaining ingredients; whirl
together. Pour this sauce over ZUCCHINI in saucepan; reheat and serve at
once. Serves 4 as side dish.

MATCHSTICKS IN SOUR CREAM

ZUCCHINI   4 cups cut in julienne strips (can be firm flesh of
very large one)
SALT   1 teaspoon
PAPRIKA   1/2 teaspoon
ONION   1, minced
VEGETABLE OIL   4 tablespoons
FLOUR   1-1/2 tablespoons
DAIRY SOUR CREAM   1-1/2 cups

Sprinkle ZUCCHINI strips with SALT; let stand for 1/2 hour. Drain and pat dry with paper towel. Sprinkle with PAPRIKA; cook with ONION in hot OIL until barely tender. Drain off OIL. In the meantime, stir FLOUR into SOUR CREAM and simmer until it thickens. Add ZUCCHINI; simmer a few minutes longer, stirring gently. Serves 6.

BEAN AND ZUCCHINI MEDLEY

ONION   1 small, chopped
VEGETABLE OIL   1 tablespoon
FRESH GREEN BEANS   1/2 pound, thinly sliced
WATER   1 tablespoon
ZUCCHINI   3 small, sliced
PARSLEY   1 tablespoon chopped
THYME   pinch
SALT and PEPPER   to taste

Cook ONIONS in OIL until golden. Add BEANS and WATER; steam 5 minutes, covered. Add rest of ingredients, cover, and steam 5 minutes or until vegetables are barely tender. Serves 4.

ZUCCHINI MARINARA

GARLIC CLOVES   2, crushed
OLIVE OIL   1 tablespoon
ANCHOVIES   6, minced
TOMATOES   2-1/2 cups canned, mashed
OREGANO   1/2 teaspoon
PARSLEY   2 tablespoons chopped
ZUCCHINI   4 cups sliced
RIPE OLIVES   sliced

In saucepan, saute GARLIC in OIL. Add ANCHOVIES, TOMATOES, OREGANO, and PARSLEY; simmer 20 minutes, stirring occasionally. Add ZUCCHINI slices; simmer until barely tender, stirring gently. Garnish with sliced RIPE OLIVES. Serves 6 to 8 as side dish.

CURRIED ZUCCHINI

ZUCCHINI   3 medium, cubed (can be firm flesh from very
              large one)
VEGETABLE OIL   1 tablespoon
GARLIC CLOVE   1, crushed
RAISINS   2 tablespoons

Curry Sauce

MARGARINE   2 tablespoons
FLOUR   2 tablespoons
WATER   1 cup
CHICKEN BOUILLON   1 cube, crushed
CURRY POWDER   1/2 teaspoon (or more to taste)
SALT
UNSWEETENED COCONUT   1/4 cup chopped

Cube ZUCCHINI into Teflon pan; saute in OIL with GARLIC and
RAISINS until barely tender. Remove ZUCCHINI to warm dish. Melt
MARGARINE in same pan; stir in FLOUR. Add WATER and
BOUILLON cube; stir until sauce becomes thick. Add CURRY POWDER
and SALT; stir. Add ZUCCHINI; simmer a minute before serving. Garnish
with COCONUT. Serves 4 as side dish.

ZUCCHINI PATTIES

ZUCCHINI   2 cups shredded (can be from large one)
ONION   1
EGG   1 whole, slightly beaten
WHEAT GERM   2 tablespoons
SALT and PEPPER   to taste
TARRAGON LEAVES   1/2 teaspoon crushed
FLOUR   2 or 3 tablespoons
VEGETABLE OIL   3 tablespoons
SEASONED SALT

Shred ZUCCHINI coarsely; drain in colander. Grate ONION coarsely. Combine all ingredients except OIL and SEASONED SALT. Use only enough FLOUR to hold mixture together. Heat OIL in large Teflon skillet (you may need more oil if not using Teflon). Drop fritter mixture, a tablespoon at a time, into OIL. Flatten with back of a spoon. Cook over medium heat until crisp brown; turn and brown on other side. Drain on paper towels; sprinkle with SEASONED SALT. Can be reheated. Serves 4.

These are delicious, actually taste "meaty" without meat.

SESAME ZUCCHINI

SESAME SEEDS   2 tablespoons
VEGETABLE OIL   2 tablespoons
LEMON JUICE   1 teaspoon
SALT   1/4 teaspoon
HOT PEPPER SAUCE   1/2 teaspoon
ZUCCHINI   2 cups cubed small (can be firm flesh of very
         large one)
PARSLEY   chopped

Brown SESAME SEEDS in OIL; add rest of seasonings and ZUCCHINI. Stir-fry until ZUCCHINI is tender-crisp. Garnish with PARSLEY. Serves 4.

SHREDDED ZUCCHINI QUICKIE

ZUCCHINI   3 cups shredded, using firm flesh of very large
         one
BUTTER or MARGARINE   1 tablespoon, melted
DAIRY SOUR CREAM   3/4 to 1 cup (or plain yogurt)
DRIED TARRAGON LEAVES   1/2 teaspoon crushed
SALT and PEPPER   to taste

Remove and discard center pulp and seeds of ZUCCHINI; shred firm flesh, about 3 cups, into saucepan. Let stand awhile to bring out juice. Add melted BUTTER; saute, stirring, for about 5 minutes. Drain. Stir in SOUR CREAM and TARRAGON; season to taste. Heat to piping hot, but do not boil. Can be kept warm in oven if necessary. Serves 6.

This is just another way to use up that whopping big zucchini.

CHEESE CUSTARD WITH ZUCCHINI

ZUCCHINI   *4 cups unpeeled and shredded*

SEASONED SALT   *1 teaspoon*

FLOUR   *1/4 cup*

WHEAT GERM   *1 tablespoon*

BAKING POWDER   *1/4 teaspoon*

MEDIUM CHEDDAR CHEESE   *1 cup shredded*

FRESHLY GROUND PEPPER   *pinch*

CHIVES   *2 tablespoons chopped*

PARSLEY   *2 tablespoons chopped*

EGGS   *3 whole*

BACON   *4 slices*

MARGARINE   *2 tablespoons, soft*

PAPRIKA

Toss ZUCCHINI with SALT, drain in colander for 1/2 hour, then press as dry as possible. Combine FLOUR, WHEAT GERM, BAKING POWDER, CHEESE, and PEPPER. Stir into ZUCCHINI. Mix in CHIVES, PARSLEY, and lightly beaten EGGS. Fry BACON until crisp; crumble. Spread 10-inch shallow casserole with soft MARGARINE; press crumbled BACON on bottom of casserole. Pour in ZUCCHINI mixture. Sprinkle with PAPRIKA. Bake at 350° for about 25 minutes, or at 325° for 30 minutes, until tests done in the middle.

EASY STUFFINGS

Start with medium-size ZUCCHINI; count 1/2 ZUCCHINI per person if used as a side dish, or 2 halves per person if it is a meat-stuffed main dish.

Steam or parboil ZUCCHINI halves until barely tender if for broiling or less-than-tender if for baking. Scoop out center pulp; either discard it or mix with stuffing.

BACON AND TOMATO SQUASHWICH

> TOMATOES
> BACON   sliced
> YELLOW CHEESE   sliced

Slice TOMATOES; cut each slice in half. Fry BACON slices until brown on 1 side only. Fill centers of scooped-out steamed ZUCCHINI with TOMATO half-slices and narrow slices of YELLOW CHEESE. Top with slices of BACON, browned side down. Broil to brown top side of BACON.

MUSHROOM

> MUSHROOMS   1/2 pound, sliced
> BUTTER   2 tablespoons, melted
> SOFT BREAD CRUMBS   1/2 cup
> MEDIUM CHEDDAR CHEESE   1/2 cup shredded
> SEASONED SALT   1 teaspoon

(Continued next page)

Saute MUSHROOMS in BUTTER; stir in BREAD CRUMBS. Add CHEESE and SALT; mix well. Pile steamed centers full of stuffing. Broil just until CHEESE is melted and tops are lightly browned.

SPINACH STUFFING

MILK   1/2 cup cold
FLOUR   2 tablespoons
FROZEN CHOPPED SPINACH   1 10-ounce package, cooked and drained
BACON   6 slices, cooked crisp and crumbled
SALT and PEPPER   to taste
MEDIUM CHEDDAR CHEESE   1/4 cup shredded

In Teflon saucepan, combine MILK and FLOUR; heat until it starts to thicken. Add drained cooked SPINACH; simmer 5 minutes. Add crumbled BACON; season to taste with SALT and PEPPER. Fill steamed halves of 3 medium ZUCCHINI; top with CHEESE. Place on greased cookie sheet and bake at 350° for 15 minutes. If desired, crumbled BACON can be used as topping with CHEESE.

MILDLY CHEESE

ONION   1/4 cup chopped
MARGARINE   2 tablespoons
MEDIUM CHEDDAR CHEESE   3/4 cup shredded
SALT   1 teaspoon
POULTRY SEASONING   1/2 teaspoon
FRESH GROUND PEPPER   1/8 teaspoon
ZUCCHINI PULP   half of what was removed from shells, chopped

Saute ONION in MARGARINE. Mix in remaining ingredients. Bake in steamed ZUCCHINI shells at 350° for 1/2 hour.

BREAD STUFFING

SOFT BREAD CRUMBS   *3 cups*
ONION   *1 small, minced*
PARSLEY   *1 tablespoon chopped*
EGGS   *2 whole, beaten*
POULTRY SEASONING   *1/2 teaspoon*
SAGE   *1/4 teaspoon*
SALT and PEPPER   *to taste*

Mix ingredients together; fill steamed halves of 3 medium ZUCCHINI. Place on oiled cookie sheet and bake at 350° for 30 minutes. Good with turkey roast or chicken. Serves 6.

BEEF STUFFED (Main Dish)

GROUND BEEF   *1/2 pound*
ONION   *1, chopped*
TOMATOES   *1 cup, drained*
DILL PICKLE   *1/4 cup chopped*
GARLIC CLOVE   *1, crushed*
CONDENSED CREAM OF MUSHROOM SOUP   *1/2 10-1/2-ounce can*
PAPRIKA   *optional*

Saute BEEF and ONION until BEEF is brown and crumbly. Add rest of ingredients. Heat all together; then fill centers. Bake at 350° for 20 minutes. For browned top, sprinkle generously with PAPRIKA.

DIETER'S SPECIAL

SEASONED SALT
LOW-FAT CHEESE

Scoop out shallow indentation in ZUCCHINI halves; sprinkle well with SEASONED SALT; top with pieces of LOW-FAT CHEESE. Broil long enough to melt CHEESE and make it bubbly.

ALMOND STUFFING

ZUCCHINI PULP
CRUMBS   buttered
SOY SAUCE   to moisten
SLIVERED ALMONDS
BUTTER
PAPRIKA

Mix ingredients together. Stuff centers; dot with BUTTER; sprinkle well with PAPRIKA. Bake at 350° for 2 minutes. (This one could also be broiled.)

BEER-BATTERED BLOSSOMS

FLOUR   5 tablespoons
BEER   1/2 cup
ZUCCHINI BLOSSOMS   12
VEGETABLE OIL
SEASONED SALT

Mix FLOUR and BEER to make batter. Dip ZUCCHINI BLOSSOMS to coat with batter; fry in OIL until golden brown; turn and brown other side. Drain on paper towels. Sprinkle with SEASONED SALT; serve hot.

Note: You can use quite a few of the male blossoms; just leave enough for good pollination. This is a good treat to fix when frost is predicted—harvest them before the frost kills them. Serves 4.

This easy batter can also be used for frying zucchini slices.

INDEX

OTHER BOOKS FROM
PACIFIC SEARCH PRESS

Asparagus: The Sparrowgrass Cookbook by Autumn Stanley
Bone Appétit! Natural Food for Pets by Frances Sheridan Goulart
Butterflies Afield in the Pacific Northwest
   by William Neill/Douglas Hepburn, photography
The Carrot Cookbook by Ann Saling
Cascade Companion by Susan Schwartz/Bob and Ira Spring,
   photography
Common Seaweeds of the Pacific Coast by J. Robert Waaland
The Crawfish Cookbook by Norma S. Upson
Cross-Country Downhill and Other Nordic Mountain Skiing
   Techniques by Steve Barnett
The Dogfish Cookbook by Russ Mohney
Fire and Ice: The Cascade Volcanoes by Stephen L. Harris
The Green Tomato Cookbook by Paula Simmons
Little Mammals of the Pacific Northwest by Ellen B. Kritzman
Living Shores of the Pacific Northwest
   by Lynwood Smith/Bernard Nist, photography
Make It and Take It: Homemade Gear for Camp and Trail
   by Russ Mohney
Messages from the Shore by Victor B. Scheffer
Minnie Rose Lovgreen's Recipe for Raising Chickens
   by Minnie Rose Lovgreen
Rhubarb Renaissance: A Cookbook by Ann Saling
The Salmon Cookbook by Jerry Dennon
Sleek & Savage: North America's Weasel Family by Delphine Haley
Spinning and Weaving with Wool by Paula Simmons
Why Wild Edibles? The Joys of Finding, Fixing, and Tasting
   by Russ Mohney
Wild Mushroom Recipes by Puget Sound Mycological Society
Wild Shrubs: Finding and Growing Your Own by Joy Spurr